Visual Factfinder

THE
LIVING
WORLD

Visual Factfinder

THE

LIVING
WORLD

BRIAN WILLIAMS

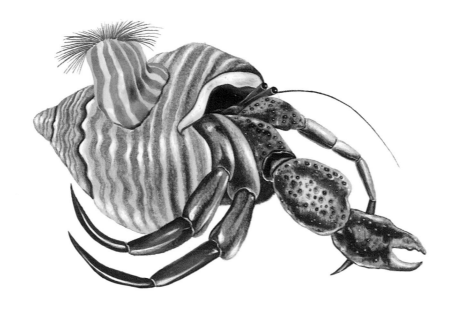

Kingfisher Books

NEW YORK

KINGFISHER BOOKS
Grisewood & Dempsey Inc.
95 Madison Avenue
New York, New York 10016

First American edition 1993
2 4 6 8 10 9 7 5 3 1 [lib. bdg.]
2 4 6 8 10 9 7 5 3 1 [pbk.]

Library of Congress Cataloging-in-Publication Data
Williams, Brian
The living world: a visual factfinder/Brian Williams – 1st
American ed.
p. cm. – (Visual factfinders)
Includes index.
Summary: Text and illustrations explore the plant and animal
kingdoms, with a separate section on the human body.
1. Natural history – Juvenile literature. 2. Body, Human – Juvenile
literature. [1. Natural history. 2 Animals. 3. Plants.
4. Body, Human.] I. Title. II. Series.
QH48.W49 1993
574 – dc20 92-41309 CIP AC

ISBN 1-85697-846-X (lib. bdg.)
ISBN 1-85697-817-6 (pbk.)

Series Editor: Michèle Byam
Assistant Editor: Cynthia O'Neill
Series Designer: Ralph Pitchford
Design Assistant: Sandra Begnor
Picture Research: Su Alexander, Elaine Willis

Additional help from Nicky Barber, Catherine Bradley,
Mark Franklin, Matthew Gore, Peter Barber,
Steve Woosnam-Savage

Printed in Spain

CONTENTS

About this Factfinder

This encyclopedic reference book gives essential facts and figures about animals, plants, and the human body, as well as such topics as evolution, habitats, and endangered species. Each topic is interpreted in a highly visual style using color illustrations and photographs that closely complement the text.

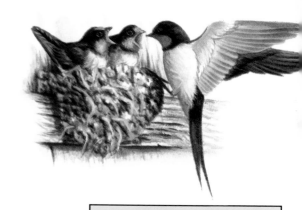

Short text essays introduce each group of plants and animals, and their different characteristics, including a separate section on the human body.

Charts and diagrams provide essential details about animal and plant classification, as well as on the physical characteristics of key species.

Captions provide in-depth information on subjects such as trees, flowers, birds, mammals, insects, fish, reptiles, and the parts of the body and its systems.

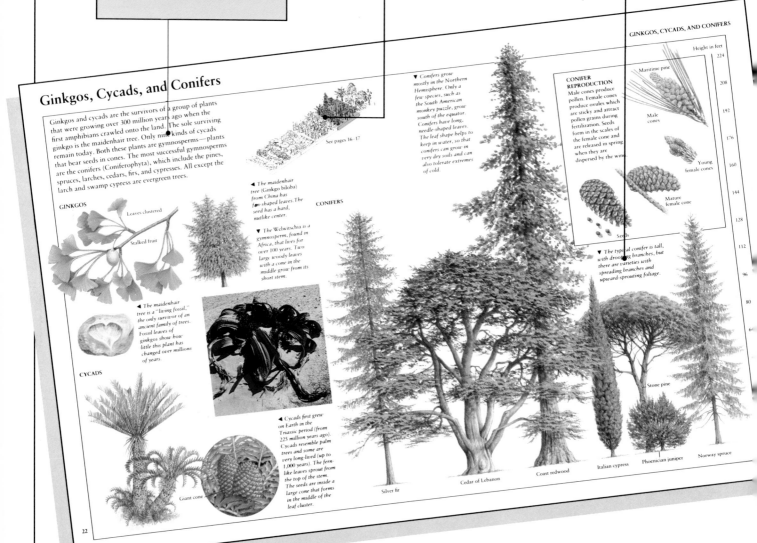

Ginkgos, Cycads, and Conifers

Ginkgos and cycads are the survivors of a group of plants that were growing over 300 million years ago when the first amphibians crawled onto the land. The sole surviving ginkgo is the maidenhair tree. Only nine kinds of cycads remain today. Both these plants are gymnosperms—plants that bear seeds in cones. The most successful gymnosperms are the conifers (Coniferophyta), which include the pines, spruces, larches, cedars, firs, and cypresses. All except the larch and swamp cypress are evergreen trees.

See pages 16–17

GINKGOS

Leaves clustered

Stalked fruit

◄ The maidenhair tree (Ginkgo biloba) from China has fan-shaped leaves. The seed has a hard, nutlike center.

◄ The maidenhair tree is a "living fossil," the only survivor of an ancient family of trees. Fossil leaves of ginkgos show how little this plant has changed over millions of years.

CYCADS

▼ The Welwitschia is a gymnosperm, found in Africa, that lives for over 100 years. Two large woody leaves with a cone in the middle grow from its short stem.

◄ Cycads first grew on Earth in the Triassic period (from 225 million years ago). Cycads resemble palm trees and some are very long-lived (up to 1,000 years). The fern-like leaves sprout from the top of the stem. The seeds are inside a large cone that forms in the middle of the leaf cluster.

Giant cone

CONIFERS

▼ Conifers grow mostly in the Northern Hemisphere. Only a few species, such as the South American monkey puzzle, grow south of the equator. Conifers have long, needle-shaped leaves. The leaf shape helps to keep in water, so that conifers can grow in very dry soils and can also tolerate extremes of cold.

GINKGOS, CYCADS, AND CONIFERS

CONIFER REPRODUCTION
Male cones produce pollen. Female cones produce ovules which are sticky and attract pollen grains during fertilization. Seeds form in the scales of the female cone and are released in spring, when they are dispersed by the wind.

Maritime pine

Male cones

Young female cones

Mature female cone

Seeds

Height in feet
224
208
192
176
160
144
128
112
96
80
64

▼ The typical conifer is tall, with drooping branches, but there are varieties with spreading branches and upward-sprouting foliage.

Silver fir

Cedar of Lebanon

Coast redwood

Italian cypress

Stone pine

Phoenician juniper

Norway spruce

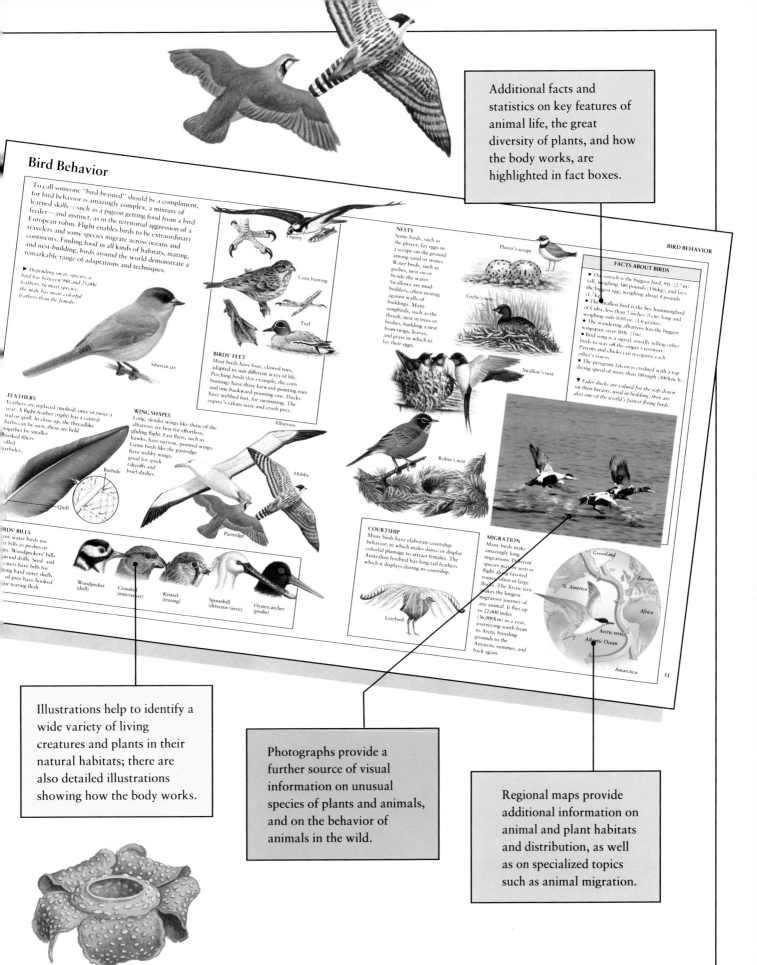

Additional facts and statistics on key features of animal life, the great diversity of plants, and how the body works, are highlighted in fact boxes.

Bird Behavior

BIRD BEHAVIOR

To call someone "bird-brained" should be a compliment, for bird behavior is amazingly complex, a mixture of learned skills—such as a pigeon getting food from a bird feeder—and instinct, as in the territorial aggression of a European robin. Flight enables birds to be extraordinary travelers and some species migrate across oceans and continents. Finding food in all kinds of habitats, mating, and nest-building, birds around the world demonstrate a remarkable range of adaptations and techniques.

Depending on its species, a bird has between 940 and 25,000 feathers. In most species, the male has more colorful feathers than the female.

Siberian jay

FEATHERS
Feathers are replaced (molted) once or twice a year. A flight feather (right) has a central rod or quill. In close-up, the threadlike barbs can be seen; these are held together by smaller hooked fibers called barbules.

Barbule

Quill

BIRDS' BILLS
Many water birds use their bills as probes or sieves. Woodpeckers' bills are wood drills. Seed-eaters have bills for cracking hard outer shells. Birds of prey have hooked bills for tearing flesh.

Woodpecker (drill)
Crossbill (nutcracker)
Kestrel (tearing)
Spoonbill (detector/sieve)
Oystercatcher (probe)

Osprey

Corn bunting

Teal

BIRDS' FEET
Most birds have four, clawed toes, adapted to suit different ways of life. Perching birds (for example, the corn bunting) have three forward-pointing toes and one backward-pointing one. Ducks have webbed feet, for swimming. The osprey's talons seize and crush prey.

WING SHAPES
Long, slender wings like those of the albatross are best for effortless, gliding flight. Fast fliers, such as hawks, have narrow, pointed wings. Game birds like the partridge have stubby wings; good for quick takeoffs and brief dashes.

Albatross

Hobby

Partridge

NESTS
Some birds, such as the plover, lay eggs in a scrape on the ground among sand or stones. Water birds, such as grebes, nest on or beside the water. Swallows are mud-builders, often nesting against walls of buildings. Many songbirds, such as the thrush, nest in trees or bushes, building a nest from twigs, leaves, and grass in which to lay their eggs.

Plover's scrape

Grebe's nest

Swallow's nest

Robin's nest

FACTS ABOUT BIRDS
- The ostrich is the biggest bird, 9ft. (2.7m) tall, weighing 340 pounds (156kg), and lays the biggest egg, weighing about 4 pounds (1.7kg).
- The smallest bird is the bee hummingbird of Cuba, less than 2 inches (5cm) long and weighing only 0.05oz. (1.6 grams).
- The wandering albatross has the biggest wingspan: over 10ft. (3m).
- Bird song is a signal, usually telling other birds to stay off the singer's territory. Parents and chicks can recognize each other's voices.
- The peregrine falcon is credited with a top diving speed of more than 180mph (300km/h).

▼ Eider ducks are valued for the soft down on their breasts, used in bedding; they are also one of the world's fastest flying birds.

COURTSHIP
Many birds have elaborate courtship behavior, in which males dance or display colorful plumage to attract females. The Australian lyrebird has long tail feathers which it displays during its courtship.

Lyrebird

MIGRATION
Many birds make amazingly long migrations. Different species may be seen in flight along favored routes, often in large flocks. The Arctic tern makes the longest migratory journey of any animal. It flies up to 22,000 miles (36,000km) in a year, journeying south from its Arctic breeding grounds to the Antarctic summer, and back again.

Greenland
Europe
N. America
Africa
Arctic tern
Atlantic Ocean
Antarctica

51

Illustrations help to identify a wide variety of living creatures and plants in their natural habitats; there are also detailed illustrations showing how the body works.

Photographs provide a further source of visual information on unusual species of plants and animals, and on the behavior of animals in the wild.

Regional maps provide additional information on animal and plant habitats and distribution, as well as on specialized topics such as animal migration.

7

Emperor penguins are remarkable parents, providing food and warmth for their chicks through the Antarctic winter.

THE
LIVING WORLD

*T*he *Living World* is an illustrated guide to the living things that inhabit the Earth. In order to appreciate the rich variety of animals and plants that make up the world's natural communities we first need to understand how life on Earth evolved, how the different species are classified, and how they have adapted to specific environments.

Plants make the Earth's atmosphere breathable; without plants there would be no animal life on Earth as we know it. We look at the fascinating world of the Plant Kingdom, from the simplest mosses to the more complex flowering plants. An equally astonishing variety of animals has evolved over the past three billion years. Each major animal group is treated separately, together with such specialized topics as animal homes, migration, relationship with people, and conservation.

Finally, *The Living World* provides a guided tour of the human body's amazing structure. We find out how the body works, and how it grows and ages. To fully appreciate the complex web of life, a wide range of essential facts and figures is provided.

Brian Williams

THE LIVING EARTH

Life on Earth

The story of life on Earth begins many millions of years before the appearance of the first human beings. From dating the rocks, we can estimate the age of the Earth at around 4.5 billion years. How life began is uncertain. It may have been due to a chemical reaction, a haphazard coming together of lifeless molecules to form a tiny organism able to reproduce itself. The oldest known forms of life are the fossils of simple bacteria and algae, over 3.5 billion years old. Today there are more than 2 million living things on our planet. Many are so microscopically tiny that they are invisible to the naked human eye. Others are giants, such as the redwood tree and the blue whale. All the kinds, or species, of plants and animals have evolved as the result of gradual adaptation to the widely differing environments the Earth offers its inhabitants.

EVOLUTION

We mark the prehistory of the Earth by eras lasting many millions of years: the Precambrian, Paleozoic, Mesozoic, and Cenozoic. Life began in the oceans over 3.5 billion years ago. The first living things were simple, single-celled organisms. Scientists are still working out the relationship between these early groups. The Paleozoic Era brought an enormous expansion of life with some animals coming out of the warm, shallow seas onto the land. The evolution of species has shaped the "family tree" of life. Many plant and animal species died out. Other species developed new forms to create the diversity of animals and plants of today.

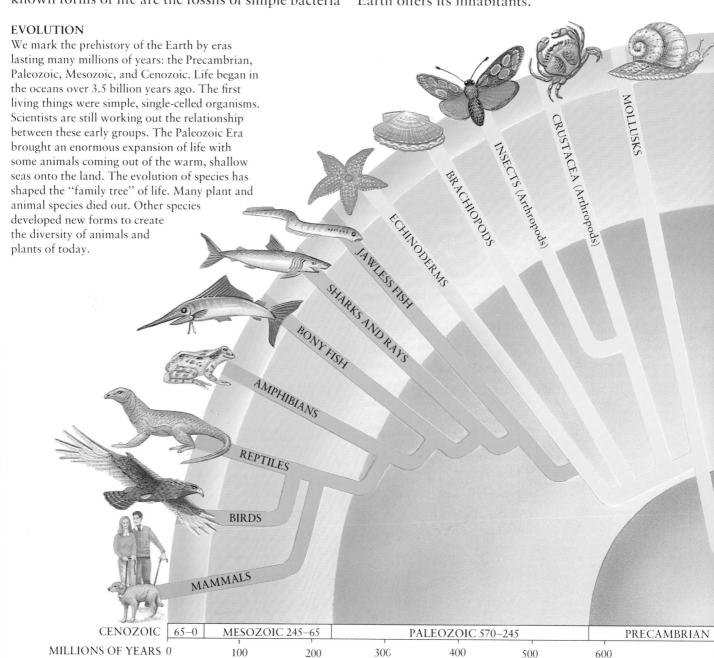

MOLLUSKS

CRUSTACEA (Arthropods)

INSECTS (Arthropods)

BRACHIOPODS

ECHINODERMS

JAWLESS FISH

SHARKS AND RAYS

BONY FISH

AMPHIBIANS

REPTILES

BIRDS

MAMMALS

CENOZOIC	65–0	MESOZOIC 245–65		PALEOZOIC 570–245			PRECAMBRIAN
MILLIONS OF YEARS	0	100	200	300	400	500	600

FOSSILS: THE EVIDENCE

Fossils like this trilobite *(left)* are the hardened remains of dead animals and plants. Fossils are found in rocks millions of years old. The earliest soft-bodied animals left no fossils. By 600 million years ago, larger and more advanced animals and plants lived in the warm seas *(above)*. These animals, which had hard shells and skeletons, left fossil remains. Dating the rocks where fossils are found fills in the calendar of life.

WORMS

COELENTERATES

SINGLE-CELLED ORGANISMS SPONGES

SINGLE-CELLED ORGANISMS

BACTERIA

FUNGI

ALGAE

MOSSES

HORSETAILS

FERNS

CYCADS

CONIFERS

FLOWERING PLANTS

PRECAMBRIAN	PALEOZOIC 570–245	MESOZOIC 245–65	65–0

600   500   400   300   200   100   0

11

Animal and Plant Classification

Classification, grouping living things together by similarities, shows how one group is related to another and how modern organisms may have evolved from earlier forms. The science of classifying plants and animals is called taxonomy, and Greek and Latin scientific names are used to identify each species, or kind, of living thing. Each species can be classed in levels: by kingdom (the largest group), then by phylum, class, order, family, genus, and lastly by species.

HOW MANY LIVING THINGS?
No one knows how many living things there are. About 2 million species have been named. But perhaps four times as many species remain unknown to science. Of the species we know about, 75 percent are animals (mostly insects), 18 percent are plants, and 7 percent are "in-betweens"— things that do not fit easily into either animal or plant groups.

ANIMAL CLASSIFICATION

KINGDOM
All animals belong to the kingdom Animalia. The other four kingdoms are Plants, Protoctists, Bacteria, and Fungi.

PHYLUM
Within the animal kingdom are 20 or more phyla. All animals with backbones belong to the phylum Chordata.

CLASS
Animals with hair on their bodies that feed their young with milk are mammals, members of the class Mammalia.

ORDER
Mammals that eat meat such as bears, dogs (including foxes), and cats, belong to the order Carnivora.

FAMILY
Dogs, foxes, and wolves look similar. These animals all belong to the same family, the Canidae.

GENUS
Animals of the same genus may not interbreed. Several foxes belong to the genus *Vulpes*.

SPECIES
Members of a species can interbreed. All fennec foxes belong to the fox species *Vulpes zerda*.

▲ *The fennec is a small fox of North Africa and Arabia. Its "family tree," from kingdom to species, is illustrated here.*

FIVE KINGDOMS

Three groups of living things are classed separately from animals and plants. Some of the simple cells are claimed to be plants and some of them are claimed to be animals. Bacteria and blue-green algae-like cells form the kingdom Bacteria. These organisms are tiny single cells. Fungi, (mushrooms and toadstools, for example), are like plants in some ways but have no chlorophyll and so cannot make their own food. Protoctists are the third "outsiders"; they contain species claimed by both botanists and zoologists and some groups with no clear relationship to any species. Some are single-celled, (such as diatoms and amoebas), and some are groups of cells, such as red and brown seaweeds.

PLANT CLASSIFICATION

KINGDOM
Every multicellular green plant, from the tiniest to the tallest, belongs to the plant kingdom.

PHYLUM
All seed plants that reproduce themselves by flowers making covered seeds are Angiosperms.

CLASS
The Angiosperms are divided into two classes, Monocotyledons and Dicotyledons (right).

ORDER
Oak trees, along with their close relatives beeches and chestnuts, belong to the order Fagales.

FAMILY
Some 900 species of trees including beeches, chestnuts, and oaks, belong to the family Fagaceae.

GENUS
All oaks belong to the genus *Quercus*. There are more than 600 species: some are tall; others are shrubby.

SPECIES
The evergreen holm oak is *Quercus ilex*. The English oak is *Quercus robur*; the American white oak is *Quercus alba*.

Turkey oak

Red oak

English oak

Oaks vary in size and in the way they grow, and each species of oak has a distinctive leaf, flower, and fruit.

Scarlet oak

13

Animal and Plant Habitats

Animals and plants live in places, or habitats, that provide the food and shelter they need. For example, giraffes (Africa), kangaroos (Australia), and prairie dogs (North America) are animals of the grasslands. Nature has equipped them to survive in this particular habitat. The Earth's regions offer many habitats, from freezing polar wastes to hot, tropical rain forests. Animals and plants live together in biological communities. Ecology is the study of how living things interact within such communities.

WORLDWIDE NATURAL REGIONS

▲ Oceans and seas form the marine habitat. The seashore, continental shelf, coral reefs, and deep, cold, ocean depths all have their own communities of plants and animals.

► Rivers and wetlands (marshes and swamps) are usually rich in plant and animal life. Animals can include fish, amphibians, reptiles, and birds such as cranes.

► Plant and animal communities are grouped worldwide into "biomes" —natural regions with similar climates and vegetation that provide similar habitats. The map shows the main land biomes. The oceans form a vast biome of their own.

◄ In tropical rain forest, plants thrive and animals (such as monkeys, birds, snakes, and insects) live in the different layers of the forest canopy.

▲ Desert plants and animals must conserve water and keep cool. Reptiles such as lizards seek shade in the midday heat. Many desert animals are small and nocturnal.

► In hot climates, savanna grasslands support herds of grazing animals, as well as the carnivores (such as African lions) that prey on these grass-eaters.

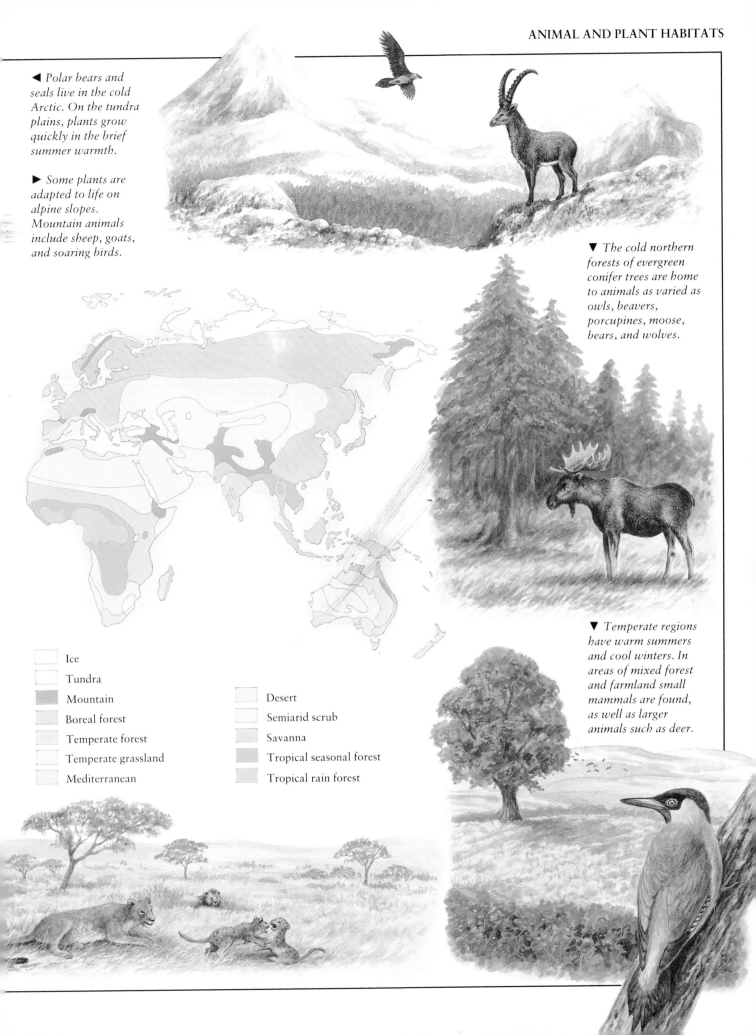

◀ Polar bears and seals live in the cold Arctic. On the tundra plains, plants grow quickly in the brief summer warmth.

▶ Some plants are adapted to life on alpine slopes. Mountain animals include sheep, goats, and soaring birds.

▼ The cold northern forests of evergreen conifer trees are home to animals as varied as owls, beavers, porcupines, moose, bears, and wolves.

Ice
Tundra
Mountain
Boreal forest
Temperate forest
Temperate grassland
Mediterranean

Desert
Semiarid scrub
Savanna
Tropical seasonal forest
Tropical rain forest

▼ Temperate regions have warm summers and cool winters. In areas of mixed forest and farmland small mammals are found, as well as larger animals such as deer.

THE PLANT KINGDOM

The World of Plants

Without plants, our planet would be a lifeless world. Plants give off the oxygen all animals need to breathe; they provide much of our food, materials such as timber and cotton, as well as many health-restoring drugs. Scientists have named more than 375,000 kinds of plants, ranging from simple algae to trees. There could be the same number of undiscovered plants growing in remote forests and on mountains. Even so, there are far fewer plants than there are animals. Some plants are widespread; others grow only in one place. Plants form the largest and longest-living things on Earth. All true plants are made up of many cells containing a material called cellulose. They develop from embryos (tiny forms of the adult plant). Most plants make their own food from water and carbon dioxide by a chemical process called photosynthesis which requires sunlight.

PLANT CLASSIFICATION

The system for naming plants and animals was drawn up by the Swedish naturalist Carl von Linné (Linnaeus) in 1758. The different groups of plants have been arranged in various ways since this time. Modern classification allows for many different phyla, of which the main ones are the ones shown here.

NEITHER ANIMALS, OR PLANTS

The Protoctists, the Bacteria, and the Fungi are not considered plants because they do not make their own food and their cells are different from those of animals and plants.

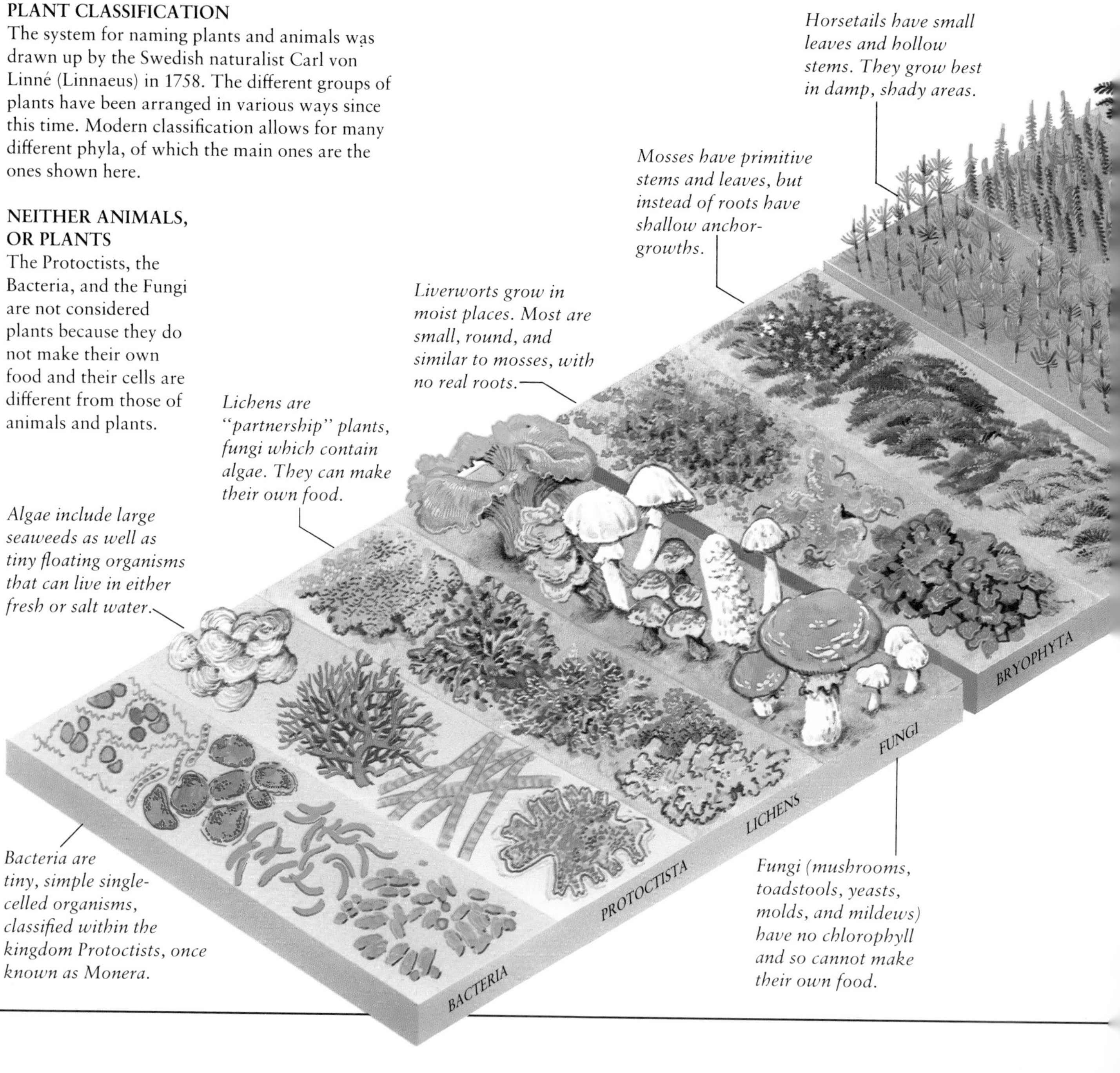

Horsetails have small leaves and hollow stems. They grow best in damp, shady areas.

Mosses have primitive stems and leaves, but instead of roots have shallow anchor-growths.

Liverworts grow in moist places. Most are small, round, and similar to mosses, with no real roots.

Lichens are "partnership" plants, fungi which contain algae. They can make their own food.

Algae include large seaweeds as well as tiny floating organisms that can live in either fresh or salt water.

Bacteria are tiny, simple single-celled organisms, classified within the kingdom Protoctists, once known as Monera.

Fungi (mushrooms, toadstools, yeasts, molds, and mildews) have no chlorophyll and so cannot make their own food.

BRYOPHYTA

FUNGI

LICHENS

PROTOCTISTA

BACTERIA

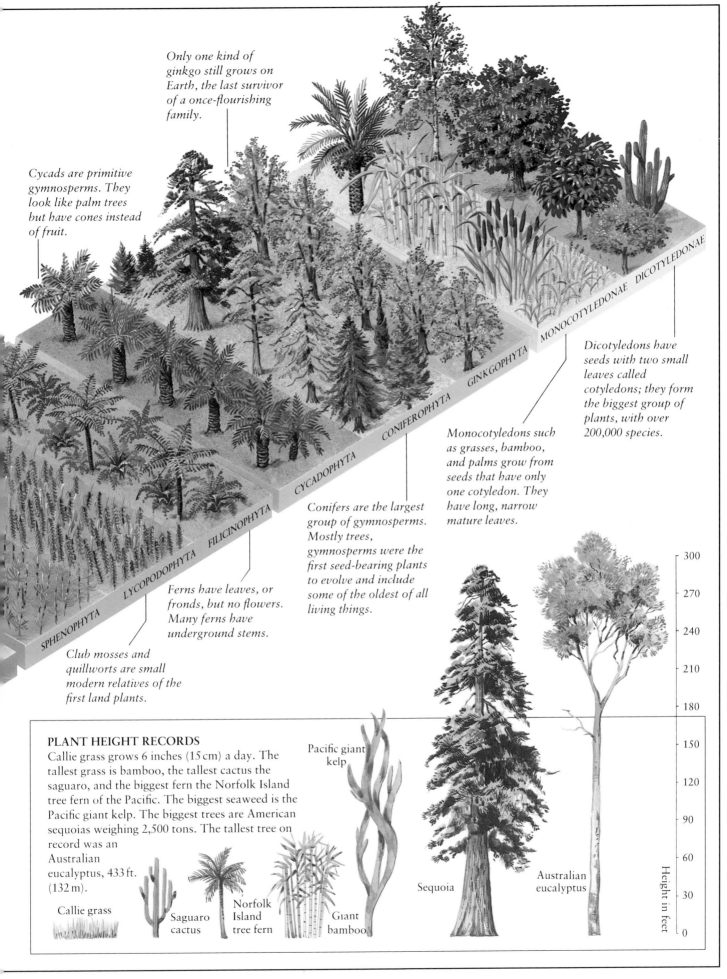

Only one kind of ginkgo still grows on Earth, the last survivor of a once-flourishing family.

Cycads are primitive gymnosperms. They look like palm trees but have cones instead of fruit.

Dicotyledons have seeds with two small leaves called cotyledons; they form the biggest group of plants, with over 200,000 species.

Monocotyledons such as grasses, bamboo, and palms grow from seeds that have only one cotyledon. They have long, narrow mature leaves.

Conifers are the largest group of gymnosperms. Mostly trees, gymnosperms were the first seed-bearing plants to evolve and include some of the oldest of all living things.

Ferns have leaves, or fronds, but no flowers. Many ferns have underground stems.

Club mosses and quillworts are small modern relatives of the first land plants.

SPHENOPHYTA

LYCOPODOPHYTA

FILICINOPHYTA

CYCADOPHYTA

CONIFEROPHYTA

GINKGOPHYTA

MONOCOTYLEDONAE

DICOTYLEDONAE

PLANT HEIGHT RECORDS

Callie grass grows 6 inches (15 cm) a day. The tallest grass is bamboo, the tallest cactus the saguaro, and the biggest fern the Norfolk Island tree fern of the Pacific. The biggest seaweed is the Pacific giant kelp. The biggest trees are American sequoias weighing 2,500 tons. The tallest tree on record was an Australian eucalyptus, 433 ft. (132 m).

Pacific giant kelp

Callie grass

Saguaro cactus

Norfolk Island tree fern

Giant bamboo

Sequoia

Australian eucalyptus

Height in feet

300
270
240
210
180
150
120
90
60
30
0

17

Bacteria, Algae, Lichens, and Fungi

These organisms are no longer classified as plants. Bacteria are tiny and single-celled, and were probably the first living things on Earth. They, and the microscopic blue-green algae, are widespread on land and in water. Other algae, classed separately as Protoctists, include the seaweeds, many of which more closely resemble plants. Fungi (mushrooms and toadstools, mildews, yeasts, and molds) are simple nongreen organisms without leaves, roots or stems; they are grouped on their own.

See pages 16–17

ALGAE

Volvox

Spirogyra

▲ Spirogyra *and* volvox *are simple organisms that live in water.* Spirogyra *grows in long strings of cells and* volvox *lives in a colony.*

Kelp

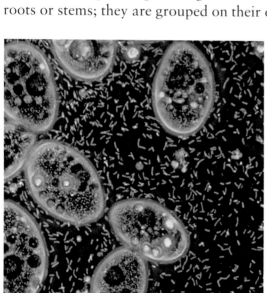

BACTERIA

Most bacteria can be seen only through a microscope. They have a simple structure, usually with a cell wall that stops them drying out. Huge numbers of bacteria live in the soil. They help to break down dead matter.

▶ *Algae include the diatoms and the seaweeds. Classed by color (green, brown, and red), the 7,000 kinds of seaweeds are plants of ocean and shore. Some have air bladders to help them float. Others cling to the seabed.*

Cockscomb   Bladderwrack   Red Rags

Shaggy ink cap
(*Coprinus comatus*)

Fly agaric
(*Amanita muscaria*)

Conical slimy cap
(*Hygrocybe conica*)

Giant puffball
(*Langermannia gigantea*)

Verdigris mushroom
(*Stopharia aeruginosa*)

Saw-gilled leptonia
(*Leptonia serrulata*)

Fairy-ring mushroom
(*Marasmius oreades*)

Parasol mushroom
(*Lepiota procera*)

Rosy earthstar
(*Geastrum rufescens*)

Field mushroom
(*Agaricus campestris*)

LICHENS

Alga

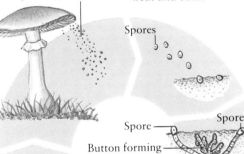

Fungal strands

Fungal mat

◀ *A lichen is made up of two living things in symbiosis, or partnership. Within the lichen is a single-celled alga enclosed in a fungus. Using photosynthesis, the alga makes food both for itself and for the fungus, which cannot survive on its own.*

▶ *Some lichens grow in soil, but most grow on rocks, walls, or tree bark. Lichens are low-growing, but can live for over 4,000 years, enduring extremes of heat and cold.*

THE LIFE CYCLE OF A FUNGUS

The mushrooms and toadstools we see are the "fruiting bodies" of fungi. The hidden part of the fungus, growing under the soil or in the wood of trees, consists of thousands of threadlike cells that form a tangled mass, the mycelium. The fruiting body appears when the fungus is ready to produce spores, which develop into new plants.

Mature mushroom disperses spores

Spores

Spore

Button forming

Spore

Mycelium

Button

FACTS ABOUT FUNGI

- A field mushroom produces 16 billion spores in just under a week.
- Raindrops help to disperse the spores of puffballs. The paper-thin outer wall of the ball encloses the powdery spores. When a raindrop hits the wall of the ball, it bulges inward and puffs out a cloud of spores.
- The most deadly fungus is the yellowish-green death cap *Amanita phalloides*, which is commonly found with beech and oak trees. If eaten, it can kill in 6 to 15 hours.

MUSHROOMS AND TOADSTOOLS

Most fungi produce fruiting bodies in autumn—a good time to spot colorful mushrooms and toadstools. Some are good to eat, but others are poisonous. Never pick or eat a mushroom until you are certain it is not poisonous.

Blood-stained bracket
(*Daedaleopsis confragosa*)

Many-zoned bracket fungus [also known as Varicolored bracket]
(*Coriolus versicolor*)

Mealy tubaria
(*Simocybe centuncula*)

Dryad's saddle
(*Polyporus squamosus*)

Yellow brain fungus
(*Tremella mesenterica*)

Devil's boletus
(*Boletus Satanas*)

Collared earthstar
(*Geastrum triplex*)

Coral spot fungus
(*Nectria cinnabarina*)

Death cap
(*Amanita phalloides*)

Common morel
(*Morchella esculenta*)

Wood blewit
(*Lepista nuda*)

Common stinkhorn
(*Phallus impudicus*)

Cystolepiota aspera
(*Lepiota friesii*)

Chanterelle
(*Cantharellus cibarius*)

Liverworts, Mosses, Horsetails, and Ferns

Mosses and liverworts are classified as the phylum Bryophyta. They are small, and instead of roots they have threadlike anchors called rhizoids. Horsetails, club mosses, and ferns were once grouped as Pteridophytes but now are three separate phyla: Sphenophyta, Lycopodophyta, and Filicinophyta. Instead of making flowers and seeds, ferns send out spores. A spore falls to the ground and grows into a "prothallus," tiny plant that makes male and female sex cells, which in turn produce the new fern plant.

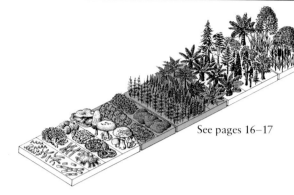

See pages 16–17

Pellia epiphylla

Marchantia polymorpha

◀ *Liverworts grow in damp places. Some have a flat body, or "thallus." Others look more leafy, with rows of leaves growing on a stem. There are about 8,000 species of liverworts, found in both hot and cold climates.*

MOSS FACTS

● Millions of years ago, ferns, horsetails, and club mosses forested the Earth.
● Peat moss is so absorbent it can be used to dress wounds.

MOSSES

Mosses are small and usually grow in clumps or dense mats, often clinging to a rock or a stone wall. As part of their complicated reproductive cycle, many mosses send out stalks with a pod at the tip. The pod releases thousands of spores to form new plants.

Sphagnum papillosum

Racomitrium lanuginosum

Leucobryum glaucum

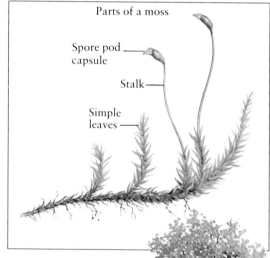

Parts of a moss

Spore pod capsule

Stalk

Simple leaves

FORMATION OF A PEAT BOG

Peat mosses are often called sphagnum mosses. They may float on top of a lake, forming a thick green carpet. This is how a peat bog starts.

The submerged parts of the moss plants die. Dead and decaying matter sinks to the bottom of the lake, forming a mat below water level.

In time, the mat of decaying vegetation builds up into a dense mass. The plant matter absorbs water and gradually turns the lake into a bog.

The lower layers are squashed by the matter above, and slowly turn into mud-like peat. The bog dries out and new plants colonize the surface.

Trees take root

Water

Dead matter falls to bottom

Moss spreads and absorbs water

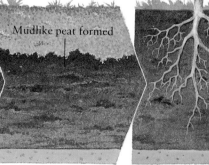

Mudlike peat formed

CLUB MOSSES

Club mosses are not true mosses. They are related to ferns. Club mosses have an underground root from which grows a stem with branches and small leaves. Club-like cones, which contain the spores from which new plants grow, form at the tips of these branches.

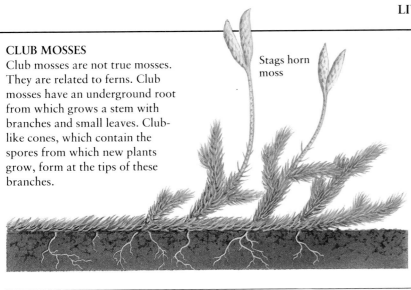

Stags horn moss

HORSETAILS

Horsetails are small plants with hollow, jointed stems and stalks that often look like miniature trees. They have no flowers and can be found in damp places.

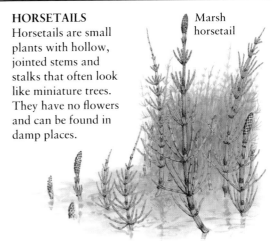

Marsh horsetail

HOW A NEW FERN GROWS

Ferns have fronds. Under each frond are spore cases, or "sporangia," lined with hundreds of spores.

The sporangia burst and spores are blown away. Fern spores survive best in shaded, moist soil. In suitable ground, a spore grows into a prothallus.

The prothallus has male and female cells from which a young fern develops; it feeds on the prothallus until it roots and can live on its own.

New fern

Fern

Sporangia

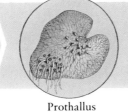

Prothallus

Young sporophyte

TYPES OF FERN

There are about 10,000 kinds of ferns on the Earth today. Tree ferns grow in the tropics. The leaves or fronds of many ferns are long and lacy. Other ferns have simple oval or round leaves.

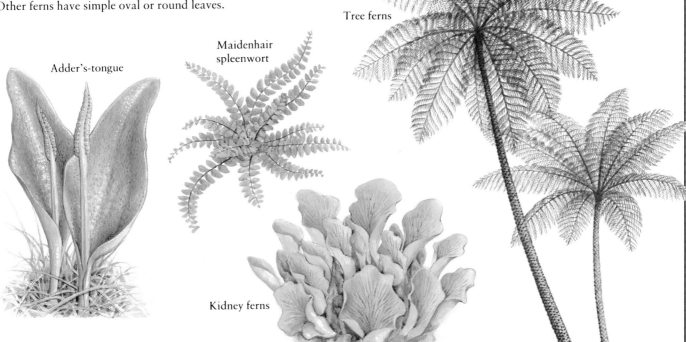

Tree ferns

Maidenhair spleenwort

Adder's-tongue

Kidney ferns

Ginkgos, Cycads, and Conifers

Ginkgos and cycads are the survivors of a group of plants that were growing over 300 million years ago when the first amphibians crawled onto the land. The sole surviving ginkgo is the maidenhair tree. Only nine kinds of cycads remain today. Both these plants are gymnosperms—plants that bear seeds in cones. The most successful gymnosperms are the conifers (Coniferophyta), which include the pines, spruces, larches, cedars, firs, and cypresses. All except the larch and swamp cypress are evergreen trees.

See pages 16–17

GINKGOS

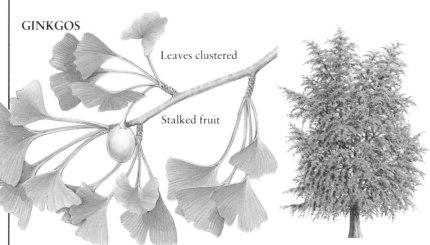

Leaves clustered

Stalked fruit

◄ *The maidenhair tree* (Ginkgo biloba) *from China has fan-shaped leaves. The seed has a hard, nutlike center.*

▼ *The* Welwitschia *is a gymnosperm, found in Africa, that lives for over 100 years. Two large woody leaves with a cone in the middle grow from its short stem.*

CONIFERS

◄ *The maidenhair tree is a "living fossil," the only survivor of an ancient family of trees. Fossil leaves of ginkgos show how little this plant has changed over millions of years.*

CYCADS

Giant cone

◄ *Cycads first grew on Earth in the Triassic period (from 225 million years ago). Cycads resemble palm trees and some are very long-lived (up to 1,000 years). The fern-like leaves sprout from the top of the stem. The seeds are inside a large cone that forms in the middle of the leaf cluster.*

Silver fir

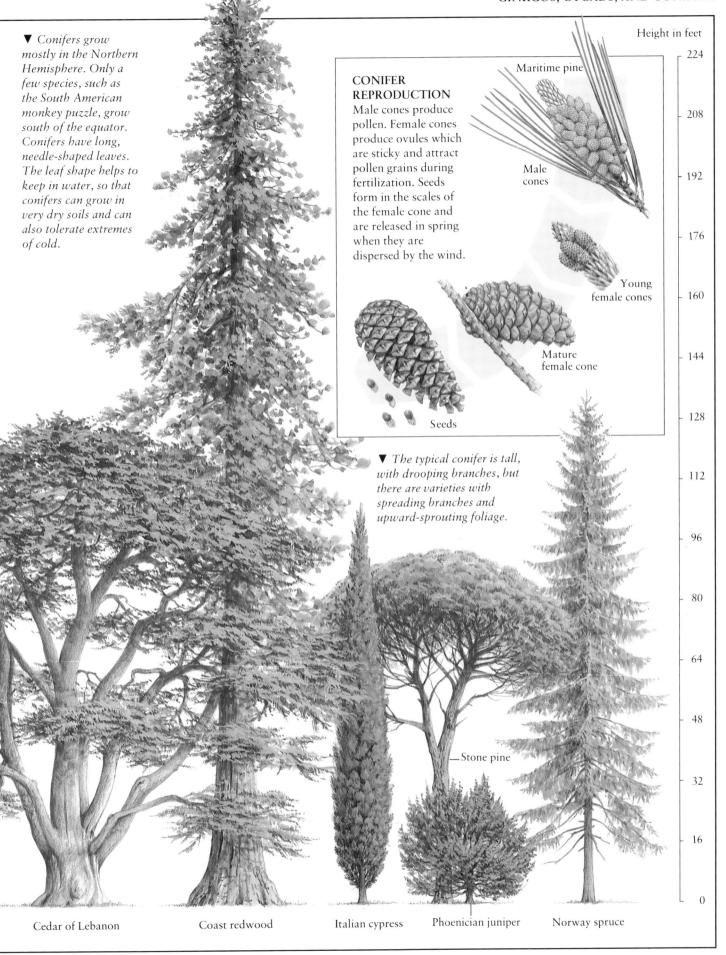

▼ Conifers grow mostly in the Northern Hemisphere. Only a few species, such as the South American monkey puzzle, grow south of the equator. Conifers have long, needle-shaped leaves. The leaf shape helps to keep in water, so that conifers can grow in very dry soils and can also tolerate extremes of cold.

Height in feet

CONIFER REPRODUCTION
Male cones produce pollen. Female cones produce ovules which are sticky and attract pollen grains during fertilization. Seeds form in the scales of the female cone and are released in spring when they are dispersed by the wind.

Maritime pine

Male cones

Young female cones

Mature female cone

Seeds

▼ The typical conifer is tall, with drooping branches, but there are varieties with spreading branches and upward-sprouting foliage.

Stone pine

224

208

192

176

160

144

128

112

96

80

64

48

32

16

0

Cedar of Lebanon   Coast redwood   Italian cypress   Phoenician juniper   Norway spruce

Monocotyledons and Dicotyledons

Monocotyledons and dicotyledons are the two classes of flowering plants. They are the most diverse of all plants, with the most efficient reproductive system in the plant world. The basic difference, which gives the two classes their names, is in the number of cotyledons, or seed leaves. Monocots have one, dicots have two. There are also differences in the mature leaves. Monocots usually have long, narrow leaves. Grass is a good example. Dicot leaves are usually broad, with smooth, rounded, or toothed edges.

See pages 16–17

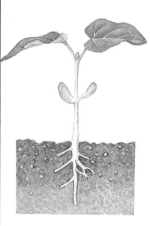

◀ *The cotyledon is the leaf part of a plant embryo, from which a new plant grows. Dicot seeds have two cotyledons.*

▶ *Monocot leaves are smooth-edged with parallel veins. The leaves grow from the base so, for example, grass keeps growing even when mowed or nibbled by animals.*

MONOCOTS	DICOTYLEDONS
The 40,000 species of monocotyledons include: **Grasses** **Cereals** such as rice, wheat, and corn **Bulb plants** such as tulips and lilies **Orchids** **Bananas** **Bulrushes and reeds** **Palm trees**	Most flowering plants are dicots. Typical examples include: **Foxgloves** **Rhododendrons** **Deciduous trees** such as oak, beech, maple **Roses, grapes** **Carrots, cucumbers** **Potatoes, beans, and peas**

▶ *Typical plants of the cool temperate forest include deciduous trees (ones that shed their leaves in autumn) such as oak, maple, and beech, and woodland flowers, such as bluebells, which bloom in spring.*

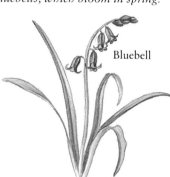

Bluebell

◀ *Grasslands are divided into three types: prairies, steppes, or savannas. Prairies have longer grasses than steppes, while savannas have trees such as palm and acacia as well as grass.*

Pampas grass

◀ *Plants such as mosses, shrubs, and flowers survive the wind and cold on high mountains by growing near the ground and having long, clinging roots. Conifers are the trees best adapted to alpine conditions.*

Alpine forget-me-not

▶ *Tropical forests contain half the known plant species. Most tropical forest trees are evergreen. Plants requiring little light, such as ferns, grow at ground level, while vines and orchids grow high in the trees.*

Rafflesia

◀ *Wetland plants include water plants such as lilies, reeds, and willow and mangrove trees. Some wetland plants live completely under water; others have air spaces in their stems, and leaves that carry air to their roots and so keep them afloat in the water.*

Giant waterlily

▶ *Plants can survive in hot deserts, although some deserts have only sand dunes. Many desert plants—cactuses, palm trees, yuccas—have spiny leaves and fleshy stems for storing water. They flower quickly after rain.*

Prickly pear

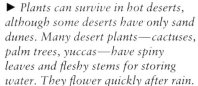

POLLINATION

A flower is the reproductive part of a seed plant. Pollen from the anther reaches the stigma. It then unites with an ovule to make a seed. Self-pollination occurs when pollen reaches a stigma on the same plant. Cross-pollination is when pollen from one plant transfers to another.

FLOWER TYPES

Flowers vary in form. Many plants produce clusters of flower heads. Some flower heads, for example, the daisy, are made up of many tiny flowers. These are called composite flowers. Three typical flower types are shown here.

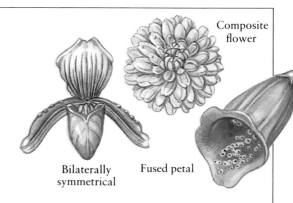

Composite flower

Bilaterally symmetrical

Fused petal

THE DEVELOPMENT OF A SEED

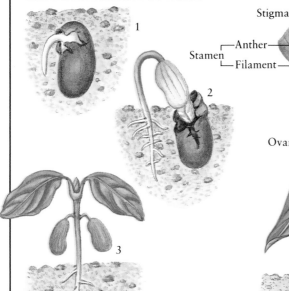

1

2

3

PARTS OF A FLOWER

Stigma

Stamen — Anther
        — Filament

Style

Ovary contains ovules

Petal

Sepals

THE LEAF

Green leaves contain chlorophyll, a substance that absorbs energy from sunlight to make food from carbon dioxide gas in the air and water in the soil. This process, unique to plants, is called photosynthesis.

Through pores, or stomata, carbon dioxide and water enter the leaf.

Stomata also give off unwanted oxygen and water.

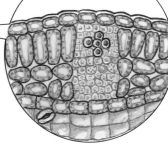

▲ First the seed absorbs water, swells and splits. It sends out an embryo root, or radicle, which pushes downward into the soil. The shoot then pushes upward, bending toward the sunlight. Finally, the first leaves sprout.

ROOTS

A plant's roots anchor it in the soil, and absorb water and minerals. Plants such as grass have a fibrous root system, with slender spreading roots; plants such as carrots have a taproot system, where one root is much larger than the rest.

▼ Plants have organs other than roots under the ground. Bulbs, tubers, corms, and rhizomes store food to help the plant survive, and produce whole new plants without sexual reproduction, as runners also do on the surface.

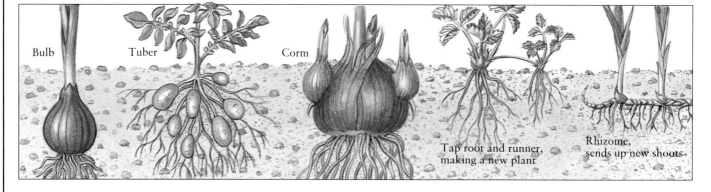

Bulb

Tuber

Corm

Tap root and runner, making a new plant

Rhizome, sends up new shoots

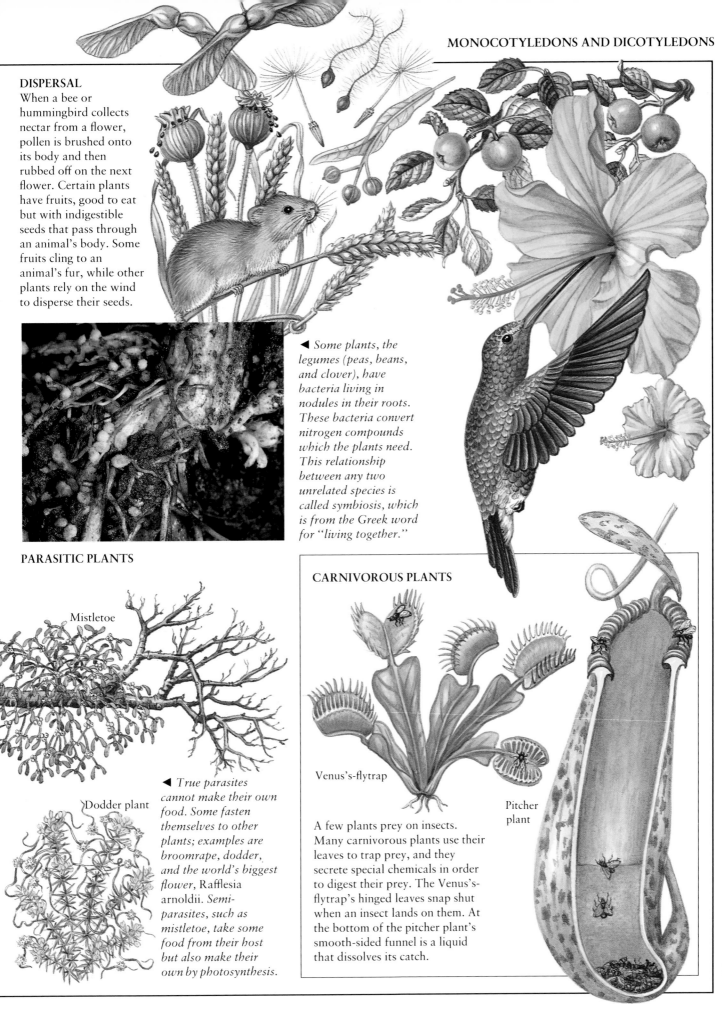

DISPERSAL

When a bee or hummingbird collects nectar from a flower, pollen is brushed onto its body and then rubbed off on the next flower. Certain plants have fruits, good to eat but with indigestible seeds that pass through an animal's body. Some fruits cling to an animal's fur, while other plants rely on the wind to disperse their seeds.

◄ Some plants, the legumes (peas, beans, and clover), have bacteria living in nodules in their roots. These bacteria convert nitrogen compounds which the plants need. This relationship between any two unrelated species is called symbiosis, which is from the Greek word for "living together."

PARASITIC PLANTS

Mistletoe

Dodder plant

◄ True parasites cannot make their own food. Some fasten themselves to other plants; examples are broomrape, dodder, and the world's biggest flower, Rafflesia arnoldii. Semi-parasites, such as mistletoe, take some food from their host but also make their own by photosynthesis.

CARNIVOROUS PLANTS

Venus's-flytrap

Pitcher plant

A few plants prey on insects. Many carnivorous plants use their leaves to trap prey, and they secrete special chemicals in order to digest their prey. The Venus's-flytrap's hinged leaves snap shut when an insect lands on them. At the bottom of the pitcher plant's smooth-sided funnel is a liquid that dissolves its catch.

27

Fruits or Vegetables?

People have many uses for plants that are most valuable as a source of food. Prehistoric people first gathered seeds, berries, and roots. About 10,000 years ago people began to grow cereals (such as wheat) and other crops. To the modern shopper, "fruit" means a juicy food, such as apples, oranges, or raspberries, grown on a bush or tree. These foods provide minerals, sugar, and vitamins. As a rule, vegetables are less sweet-tasting. The part of the plant that we eat may be its leaf, stem, root, seed, or fruit.

WHAT PARTS DO WE EAT?

BULB	Onion, garlic
TUBER	Potato, Jerusalem artichoke, yam, cassava
ROOT	Carrot, parsnip, beet, radish, turnip, Swedish turnip, sweet potato
LEAF	Brussels sprouts, cabbage, chard, Chinese cabbage, watercress, endive, kale, lettuce, spinach
FLOWER	Broccoli, cauliflower
FRUIT	Cucumber, zucchini, eggplant, apple, pepper, pumpkin, tomato, watermelon
NUT	Coconut, almond, chestnut, filbert, pistachio, pine nut, cashew
SEED	Brazil nut, peanut, bean, pea, lentil, corn, rice, oats, wheat, sunflower seed
STEM	Asparagus, kohlrabi, bamboo shoots, green onions. Celery and rhubarb are leafstalks

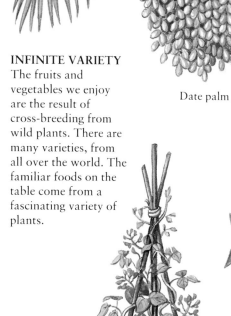

INFINITE VARIETY
The fruits and vegetables we enjoy are the result of cross-breeding from wild plants. There are many varieties, from all over the world. The familiar foods on the table come from a fascinating variety of plants.

Date palm

Bean

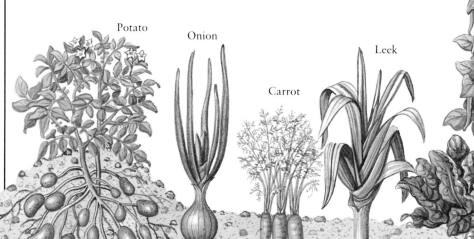

Potato

Onion

Carrot

Leek

Spinach

Cauliflower

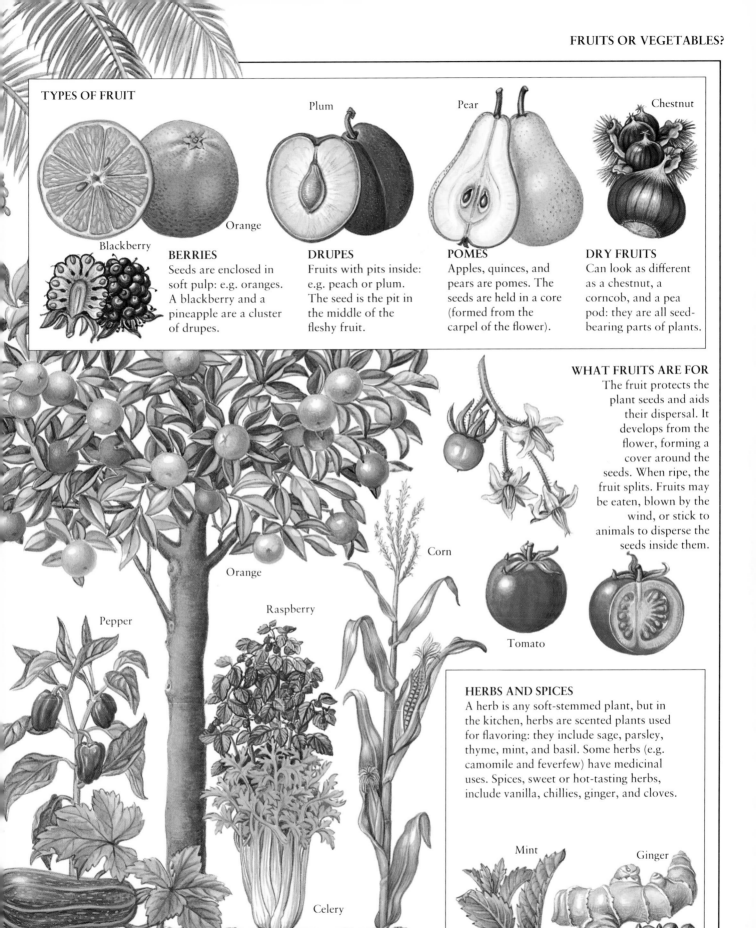

TYPES OF FRUIT

Plum

Pear

Chestnut

Orange

Blackberry

BERRIES
Seeds are enclosed in soft pulp: e.g. oranges. A blackberry and a pineapple are a cluster of drupes.

DRUPES
Fruits with pits inside: e.g. peach or plum. The seed is the pit in the middle of the fleshy fruit.

POMES
Apples, quinces, and pears are pomes. The seeds are held in a core (formed from the carpel of the flower).

DRY FRUITS
Can look as different as a chestnut, a corncob, and a pea pod: they are all seed-bearing parts of plants.

WHAT FRUITS ARE FOR
The fruit protects the plant seeds and aids their dispersal. It develops from the flower, forming a cover around the seeds. When ripe, the fruit splits. Fruits may be eaten, blown by the wind, or stick to animals to disperse the seeds inside them.

Orange

Corn

Pepper

Raspberry

Tomato

HERBS AND SPICES
A herb is any soft-stemmed plant, but in the kitchen, herbs are scented plants used for flavoring: they include sage, parsley, thyme, mint, and basil. Some herbs (e.g. camomile and feverfew) have medicinal uses. Spices, sweet or hot-tasting herbs, include vanilla, chillies, ginger, and cloves.

Mint

Ginger

Celery

Squash

Cloves

Trees

There are two main groups of trees, conifers (softwoods) and broadleaf trees (hardwoods). Conifers carry their leaves all year round, as do many tropical trees. Broadleaf trees in cooler climates are deciduous: they shed their leaves in the fall. Trees need more internal stiffening than smaller plants. In trees the tubes called xylem, which carry water through the stem (or trunk) from the roots, are thick and stiffened. Thinner-walled tubes called phloem carry food made in the leaves to other parts of the plant.

▼ *Most deciduous trees have broad, flat leaves. They may be oval, with smooth or toothed edges. Others are narrow (peach), pinnate—compound —(acacia or ash), and forked (horse chestnut or sycamore).*

Horse chestnut

Sycamore

False acacia

FALLING LEAVES

Losing their leaves in autumn helps deciduous trees to conserve water in winter. Food "pipes" to the stem are sealed: food is stored for next year's bud. The leaf is sealed off from the stem; the chlorophyll that makes the leaf green breaks down and hidden colors are seen.

Bud

Cork layer

Dead leaf

DEEP ROOTS

Roots take in water and minerals. Some trees have long roots, with as much growth below the ground as above it. Others have massive trunks, but shallow roots.

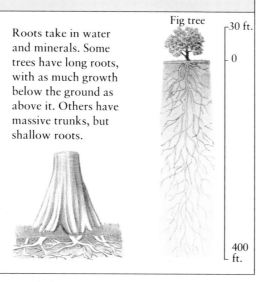

Fig tree

30 ft.

0

400 ft.

Peach

Silver birch

Judas tree

DECIDUOUS TREES

Most broadleaf trees are deciduous, although some tropical broadleaves are evergreen. A typical broadleaf tree has spring flowers, which develop into fruits, and a spreading crown and roots.

Spruce

Fir

Monkey puzzle

Larch

Cypress

▶ *All conifer tree species have cones and needles, but these vary considerably. When the cone has ripened, the seeds inside it are dispersed.*

INSIDE A TREE

Annual growth rings are seen when a tree is cut. The outer bark, or cork layer, forms a hard, dead tissue that protects the living inner part of the tree; it stretches to let the trunk and branches grow more thickly. The inner bark, or phloem, carries food through tiny pipelines. The inner wood, or xylem, also consists of pipelines that carry water, known as sap, from the root to the leaves; its task is to make the roots, trunk, and branches grow more quickly.

Cross section through a tree trunk

Bark

Phloem

Xylem

CONIFEROUS TREES

Conifers, or needle-leaf trees, rarely drop their leaves. They do not have flowers, but produce seeds in cones. Most are evergreen. A typical conifer has shallow roots and drooping branches.

FACTS ABOUT TREES

◀ *The banyan tree of India grows aerial roots, wide enough to shelter a small army. One in Sri Lanka has 3,300 trunks.*

▲ *The bristlecone pine is the oldest living tree. Some bristlecones are over 4,000 years old.*

▶ *Bonsai is the ancient Japanese art of growing miniature trees. The trees are grown in pots or trays, and kept small by pruning and shaping them.*

▲ *The baobab of Africa and Australia has a bottle-shaped trunk.*

31

Plants and People

Plants are important to us, both as sources of food and as raw materials. About 10,000 years ago people began to grow plants, rather than simply collecting them from the wild. The basic food crops, such as cereals, were developed in this way by selective breeding from wild plants. Today, cultivated plants may look very different from their wild ancestors, and genetic engineering is making it possible to develop plants that yield large crops, resist pests, and grow in unfavorable conditions.

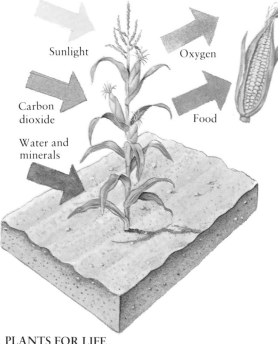

Sunlight

Oxygen

Carbon dioxide

Food

Water and minerals

THE USES OF PLANTS

Many different parts of plants can be used. The sap of the rubber tree is tapped to give the latex from which natural rubber is made. Cotton comes from the ripe fruit, or "bolls," of the cotton plant. Inside the boll is a mass of fibers enclosing the seeds. Cork comes from the bark of the Mediterranean cork oak. The cork is stripped from the tree once every nine or ten years.

Tire

Rubber tree being tapped

Cotton thread

Cork oak

Cotton plant

Cotton T-shirt

Cork

PLANTS FOR LIFE

Plants are essential to life on Earth. The chlorophyll in the leaves of green plants absorbs light energy from the Sun. Water is drawn up through the roots and carbon dioxide gas taken in from the air by the leaves, combining to make glucose (sugar) and oxygen. The plants use the sugar for food, releasing the oxygen into the air.

▶ *All animals depend on plants for their food in some way. The most important food crops grown by people include wheat, corn, rice, potatoes, beans, cassava, fruits, and vegetables.*

FACTS ABOUT PLANTS AND PEOPLE

- The painkilling drug morphine is made from the opium poppy.
- Quinine, once used for treating malaria, comes from the cinchona tree.
- The drug digitalis, a treatment for heart disease, comes from the leaves of the foxglove.
- The first antibiotic drug effective against infections was penicillin. It was developed in the 1940s from a mold found in 1928 growing in a dish that contained bacteria. The mold killed the bacteria.

Cinchona tree (flower of)

HOW PEOPLE CHANGE PLANTS

There are thousands of varieties of apples, developed over the past 2,000 years. Most apple trees are grown from a bud of one variety grafted onto the roots of another. Plant breeders have also cross-bred flowers such as roses to give them better colors or perfumes.

Cox apple

Golden Delicious apple

Hyb rose

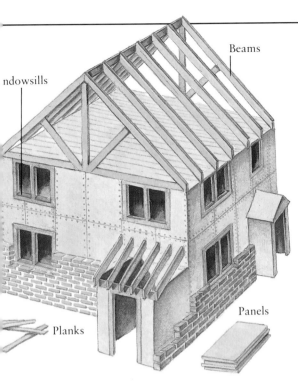

Beams

ndowsills

Planks

Panels

▲ *Timber for building use is mostly sawn softwood planking or factory-made laminate (such as plywood) and chipboard. Softwoods are far easier to saw, plane, and bore than hardwoods, making them ideal for the frame of a house. However, hardwoods such as oak or maple are often used for a house's interior paneling and for finished floors.*

HARDWOODS AND SOFTWOODS

These terms refer to the trees from which timber comes, not to its hardness. Softwood comes from conifer trees such as pine and cedar. Hardwood comes from broadleaf trees growing either in cool regions (trees such as oak and ash) or in the tropics (trees such as mahogany and ebony).

THE USES OF HARDWOOD

Hardwoods can be very strong. Oak, for example, was used to make sailing ships. Beech is hard-wearing and elm is water-resistant. Furniture made from tropical hardwoods has an attractive color.

THE USES OF SOFTWOOD

Softwoods grow quickly, and are easy to cut and shape by hand or on machines. They are used for making boxes, furniture, toys, and for building materials such as planks, frames, doors, posts, and beams.

▲ *Most paper is made from the pulp of trees such as beech, fir, pine, and oak, although other plant fibers can also be pulped to make paper.*

▶ *Fine furniture is made from woods with a distinctive grain, such as cherry and walnut.*

▶ *Reeds and grasses have been used for thousands of years as materials for house-building and in basket-making.*

PLANTS AND LANDSCAPE

People have changed complete landscapes by cutting down forests *(above)*, plowing prairies, and by introducing new kinds of plants. Plants are a vital ingredient of our landscape. Planting trees makes cities more pleasant to live in, and screens busy roads or factories.

DANGEROUS PLANTS

Some food plants have parts that are dangerous to eat—rhubarb and potato leaves, for example. Certain mushrooms are harmful if eaten. Poison ivy contains an irritant oil. Every part of the azalea, deadly nightshade, foxglove, oleander, and rhododendron is poisonous. Yew and laburnum seeds are poisonous, as are the berries of mistletoe and the bulb of a hyacinth.

Smooth lepiota *Leucoagaricus naucinus* (poisonous)

Field mushroom *Agaricus campestris* (edible)

Hemlock

Rhubarb leaves

THE ANIMAL KINGDOM

The World of Animals

What makes an animal? A general rule is that animals move (plants are anchored by their roots). Unlike most plants, which make their own food, animals must eat either plants or other animals. Some live on dry land, others in water. Some have two legs, others have four, six, eight, or hundreds. Some are constantly warm-blooded; others have body temperatures that vary with their surroundings. Animals with similar body characteristics are grouped together. Scientists do this to identify each distinct species, and also to show how species are related within larger groups. Common features reveal how animal species have evolved over millions of years. An elephant looks very different from a dog, yet both are mammals and they share with birds, fish, amphibians, and reptiles an important body feature—a backbone of vertebrae.

THE ANIMAL KINGDOM
There are over one million animal species, classified into 20 or more phyla. For example, all animals with backbones (vertebrates) belong to the phylum Chordata. This includes all reptiles, birds, and mammals, but even so, the chordates make up only a small part of the vast animal kingdom. Only major phyla are shown here.

Protozoans are single-celled organisms. They move by floating or waving hairlike organs on their bodies. Protozoans are now usually classed in the separate Protoctist kingdom.

Sponges are the most primitive of multi-cellular animals; the 5,000 species make up the phylum Porifera. Sponges live in either fresh water or oceans; like most animals, they eat their food but they cannot move from place to place.

Flatworms, flukes, and tapeworms belong to the phylum Platyhelminthes. These animals have soft, thin, flat bodies. Most flatworms live as parasites in other animals.

Nematodes are thin, round worms. Some are too small to be seen without a microscope. There are more than 15,000 species, living in soil and water. Many, such as hookworms, are parasites.

Worms with long bodies made up of segments are annelids. They are all soft-bodied, without hard skeletons. This phylum includes earthworms, leeches, and _____ lugworms.

Coelenterates or Cnidaria include jellyfish, coral polyps, and sea anemones. There are about 9,500 species, commonly found in the oceans. Freshwater species are less common.

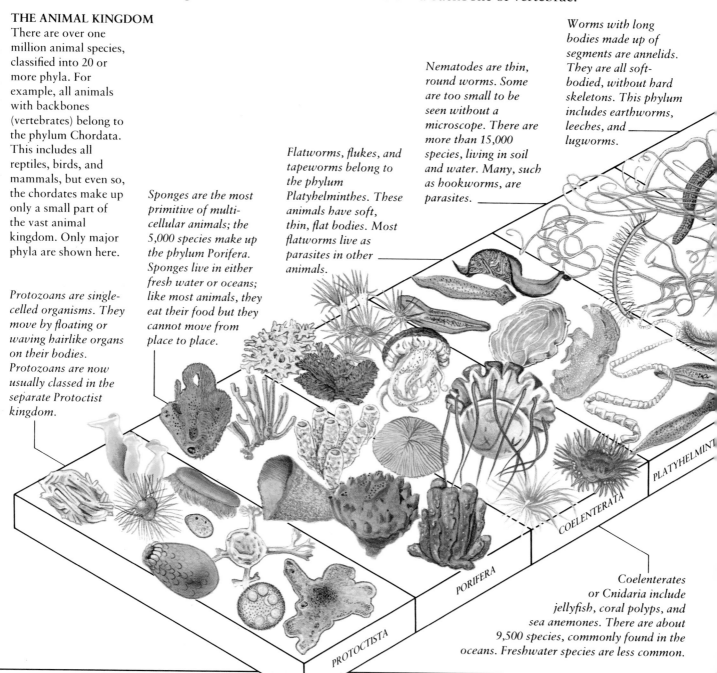

PROTOCTISTA

PORIFERA

COELENTERATA

PLATYHELMINT

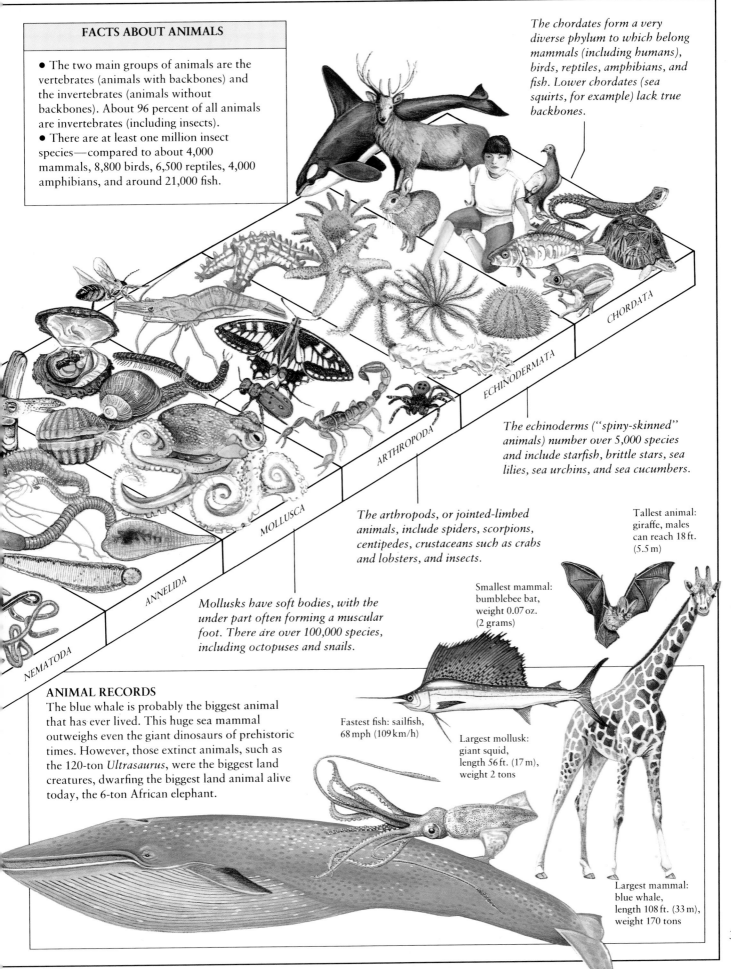

FACTS ABOUT ANIMALS

• The two main groups of animals are the vertebrates (animals with backbones) and the invertebrates (animals without backbones). About 96 percent of all animals are invertebrates (including insects).

• There are at least one million insect species—compared to about 4,000 mammals, 8,800 birds, 6,500 reptiles, 4,000 amphibians, and around 21,000 fish.

The chordates form a very diverse phylum to which belong mammals (including humans), birds, reptiles, amphibians, and fish. Lower chordates (sea squirts, for example) lack true backbones.

CHORDATA

ECHINODERMATA

ARTHROPODA

MOLLUSCA

ANNELIDA

NEMATODA

The echinoderms ("spiny-skinned" animals) number over 5,000 species and include starfish, brittle stars, sea lilies, sea urchins, and sea cucumbers.

The arthropods, or jointed-limbed animals, include spiders, scorpions, centipedes, crustaceans such as crabs and lobsters, and insects.

Mollusks have soft bodies, with the under part often forming a muscular foot. There are over 100,000 species, including octopuses and snails.

Tallest animal: giraffe, males can reach 18 ft. (5.5 m)

Smallest mammal: bumblebee bat, weight 0.07 oz. (2 grams)

ANIMAL RECORDS

The blue whale is probably the biggest animal that has ever lived. This huge sea mammal outweighs even the giant dinosaurs of prehistoric times. However, those extinct animals, such as the 120-ton *Ultrasaurus*, were the biggest land creatures, dwarfing the biggest land animal alive today, the 6-ton African elephant.

Fastest fish: sailfish, 68 mph (109 km/h)

Largest mollusk: giant squid, length 56 ft. (17 m), weight 2 tons

Largest mammal: blue whale, length 108 ft. (33 m), weight 170 tons

Marine Invertebrates, Worms, Snails, and Slugs

The first multi-celled animals were sea-living invertebrates, creatures without backbones that swam and crawled in the oceans millions of years before the first backboned animals (fish). Their modern descendants include worms, corals, clams, snails, starfish, and squid. Even without the arthropods (for example, insects, spiders, and crabs), these "lower" animals are enormously successful: there are more than 100,000 mollusks, ranging from tiny snails to giant squid, and several thousand kinds of worms.

See pages 34–35

FACTS ABOUT MARINE INVERTEBRATES

- The bootlace worm of the North Sea can grow up to 180 ft. (55 m) long.
- Sea cucumbers (echinoderms) force out their own insides to confuse enemies, while they crawl to safety.
- The venom of a sea wasp jellyfish can kill a person in 1 to 3 minutes.
- The biggest snail is the African giant snail, weighing 2 lb. (900 grams).
- The quahog clam of the Atlantic Ocean can live for 220 years.
- Squids, cuttlefish, and octopuses are the most active mollusks. They are carnivores, and swim rapidly by squirting out jets of water behind them.

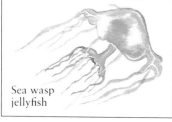

Sea wasp jellyfish

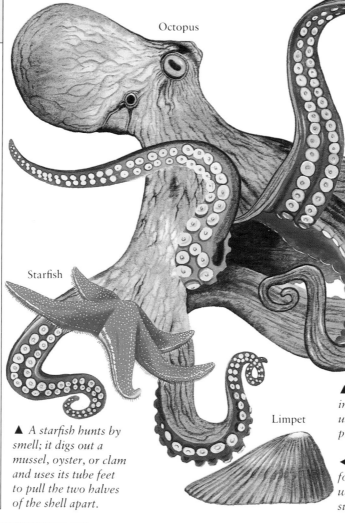

Octopus

Starfish

Limpet

▲ A starfish hunts by smell; it digs out a mussel, oyster, or clam and uses its tube feet to pull the two halves of the shell apart.

▲ The octopus is the most intelligent of the mollusks. It uses its sucker arms to seize prey, and kills with a bite.

◄ Limpets cling to rocks. A force 2,000 times the limpet's weight is needed to dislodge its suckerlike foot.

► Coral reefs are only found in tropical seas, as the corals that form the reefs cannot live in cold water. Coral is made of limestone formed by millions of tiny marine animals.

◄ Small fish feed and shelter among the colorful branches and fronds of coral.

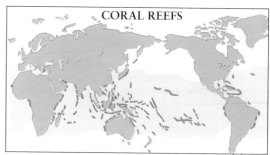

CORAL REEFS

〜 Coral reefs

☐ 70°F (coral cannot survive below this temperature)

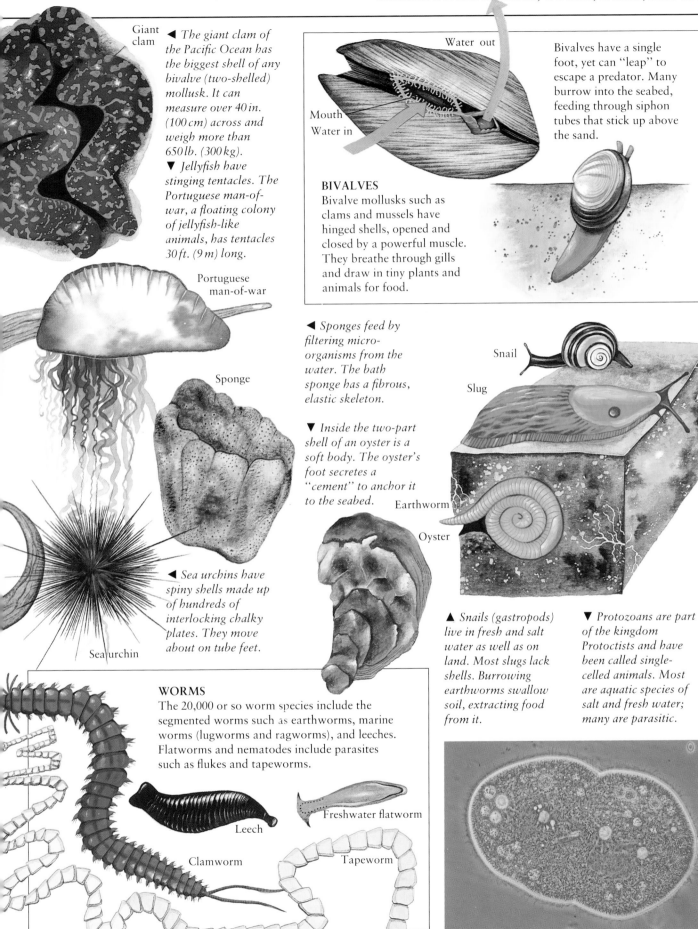

Giant clam

◄ *The giant clam of the Pacific Ocean has the biggest shell of any bivalve (two-shelled) mollusk. It can measure over 40 in. (100 cm) across and weigh more than 650 lb. (300 kg).*

▼ *Jellyfish have stinging tentacles. The Portuguese man-of-war, a floating colony of jellyfish-like animals, has tentacles 30 ft. (9 m) long.*

Water out

Mouth
Water in

Bivalves have a single foot, yet can "leap" to escape a predator. Many burrow into the seabed, feeding through siphon tubes that stick up above the sand.

BIVALVES
Bivalve mollusks such as clams and mussels have hinged shells, opened and closed by a powerful muscle. They breathe through gills and draw in tiny plants and animals for food.

Portuguese man-of-war

◄ *Sponges feed by filtering micro-organisms from the water. The bath sponge has a fibrous, elastic skeleton.*

Snail

Slug

▼ *Inside the two-part shell of an oyster is a soft body. The oyster's foot secretes a "cement" to anchor it to the seabed.*

Sponge

Earthworm

Oyster

◄ *Sea urchins have spiny shells made up of hundreds of interlocking chalky plates. They move about on tube feet.*

Sea urchin

▲ *Snails (gastropods) live in fresh and salt water as well as on land. Most slugs lack shells. Burrowing earthworms swallow soil, extracting food from it.*

▼ *Protozoans are part of the kingdom Protoctists and have been called single-celled animals. Most are aquatic species of salt and fresh water; many are parasitic.*

WORMS
The 20,000 or so worm species include the segmented worms such as earthworms, marine worms (lugworms and ragworms), and leeches. Flatworms and nematodes include parasites such as flukes and tapeworms.

Leech

Freshwater flatworm

Clamworm

Tapeworm

Millipedes, Crabs, and Spiders

Like insects, these animals are arthropods, members of the largest animal phylum. All arthropods have jointed limbs and most have a plated body-covering, which the animal molts, or sheds, as it grows. Centipedes and millipedes are wormlike, with a pair of limbs on almost every segment of their bodies. Crustaceans (for example, crabs, lobsters, and woodlice) number more than 30,000 species. The biggest group, with over 50,000 species, is the arachnids: spiders, scorpions, and mites.

See pages 34–35

FACTS ABOUT ARTHROPODS

- The first true arthropods lived in the sea. They were the trilobites, now extinct.
- Millipedes use chemical defenses. Stink glands in their bodies secrete a venom capable of killing or repelling insects.
- Most crabs live in the oceans and seas, but robber crabs are so adapted to life on land that they drown if kept under water.

Centipede

◀ *Millipedes have even more legs than centipedes: as many as 375 pairs. They live in soil and leaf litter, feeding on decaying vegetation.*

Millipede

▼ *The horseshoe, or king, crab is closer to spiders than to true crabs. Up to 2 ft. (60 cm) long, it has a horny shield.*

◀ *Not all centipedes have 100 legs; some have as few as 30, others as many as 177. They are all fast-moving hunters with poisonous claws.*

▼ *Lobsters are the heaviest crustaceans, weighing up to 44 pounds (20 kg). Spiny lobsters migrate in long columns.*

Horseshoe crab

Lobster

LIFE CYCLE OF A SHRIMP

Marine crustaceans such as shrimps lay eggs, often carried by the female until they hatch. The tiny larvae look very different from the adults. The larvae drift through the water, gradually changing body shape until fully developed.

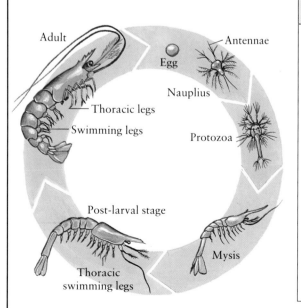

Adult

Egg

Antennae

Nauplius

Thoracic legs

Swimming legs

Protozoa

Post-larval stage

Mysis

Thoracic swimming legs

CARING PARENTS

Few arthropods are caring parents. The arthropods that show most concern for their young are those with the fiercest reputations as killers: spiders and scorpions. A female scorpion gives birth to live young. She carries the babies around on her back until after their first molt.

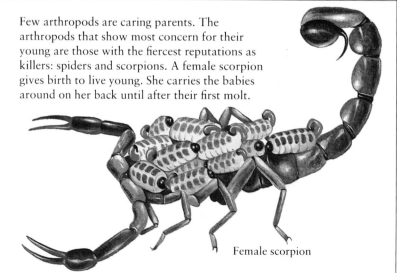

Female scorpion

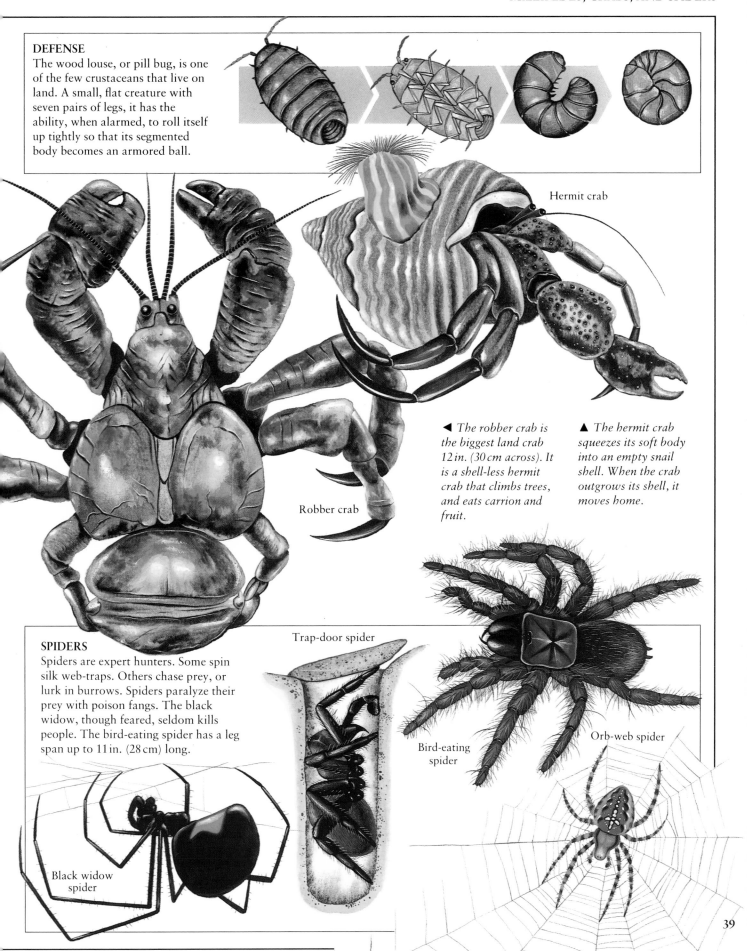

DEFENSE

The wood louse, or pill bug, is one of the few crustaceans that live on land. A small, flat creature with seven pairs of legs, it has the ability, when alarmed, to roll itself up tightly so that its segmented body becomes an armored ball.

Hermit crab

◀ *The robber crab is the biggest land crab 12 in. (30 cm across). It is a shell-less hermit crab that climbs trees, and eats carrion and fruit.*

▲ *The hermit crab squeezes its soft body into an empty snail shell. When the crab outgrows its shell, it moves home.*

Robber crab

SPIDERS

Spiders are expert hunters. Some spin silk web-traps. Others chase prey, or lurk in burrows. Spiders paralyze their prey with poison fangs. The black widow, though feared, seldom kills people. The bird-eating spider has a leg span up to 11 in. (28 cm) long.

Trap-door spider

Bird-eating spider

Orb-web spider

Black widow spider

Insects

There are about one million known species of insects, and millions more are probably still to be identified; about 80 percent of all known animals are insects. Some scientists believe there could be as many as 10 million insect species. The secret of the insects' success is their adaptability. Although they are limited in size by their body design, they have conquered all environments, from the hottest to the coldest places. Evolution has also equipped them to eat an astonishing variety of foods.

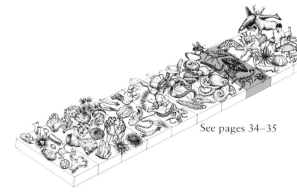

See pages 34–35

FACTS ABOUT INSECTS

- Insects breathe through tiny holes called "spiracles" along the sides of their bodies. Each hole allows air to pass into a system of tubes branching all around the insect's body. These tubes carry oxygen to the cells and carry away carbon dioxide.
- Many insects can lift or drag an object 20 times their own weight. A caterpillar has from 2,000 to 4,000 muscles—six times as many as a human.
- Botflies and horseflies can fly at 24 mph (39 km/h). A tiny midge holds the record for fast wing beats: more than 62,000 times a minute.

Midge

THE BODIES OF INSECTS

All insects, like this honeybee, have three pairs of legs. An insect's body has three parts: a head, a middle, or thorax, where the legs are attached, and an abdomen. Most adult insects have wings and a pair of antennae. But while the majority of insects (like the bee) have four wings, flies only have two.

▼ *Hornets are large social wasps. They build nests of paper made from chewed-up plant matter. Hornets sting if disturbed, and hunt flies and caterpillars.*

▶ *Dragonflies are the fastest insects, with a top speed of over 34 mph (55 km/h).*

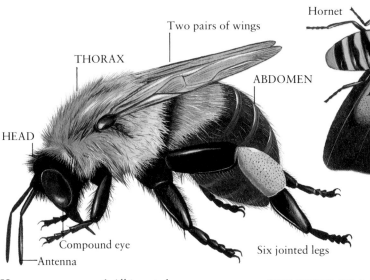

Two pairs of wings

THORAX

ABDOMEN

Hornet

HEAD

Compound eye

Antenna

Six jointed legs

▲ *The largest insect is the Queen Alexandra birdwing butterfly of Papua New Guinea – 11 in. (28 cm) from wingtip to wingtip.*

LIFE CYCLE OF A MOTH

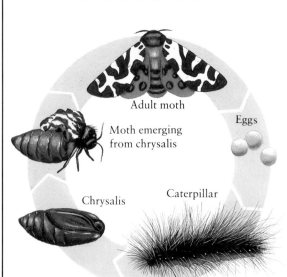

Adult moth

Moth emerging from chrysalis

Eggs

Chrysalis

Caterpillar

◀ *All insects lay eggs. The young of most insects go through four stages of growth and development. A moth develops from egg to caterpillar (larva) to chrysalis before emerging as an adult.*

▶ *Grasshoppers and insects such as cockroaches, earwigs, and aphids, go through three stages of growth. After hatching from the egg, the young look like miniature adults, though at first they lack wings.*

LIFE CYCLE OF A GRASSHOPPER

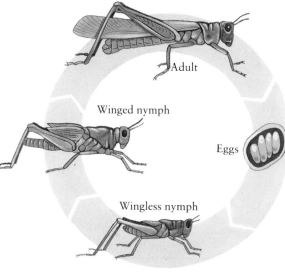

Adult

Winged nymph

Eggs

Wingless nymph

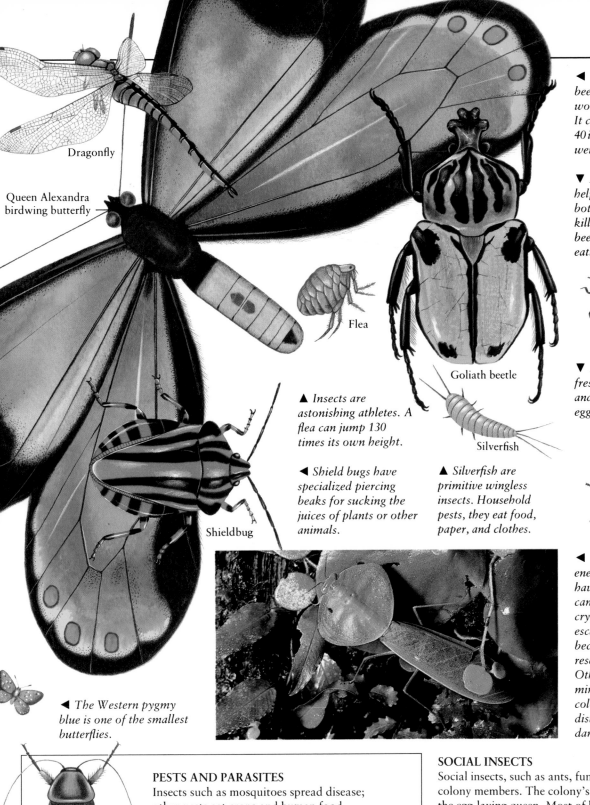

Dragonfly

Queen Alexandra
birdwing butterfly

Flea

Goliath beetle

Silverfish

Shieldbug

▲ *Insects are astonishing athletes. A flea can jump 130 times its own height.*

◀ *Shield bugs have specialized piercing beaks for sucking the juices of plants or other animals.*

▲ *Silverfish are primitive wingless insects. Household pests, they eat food, paper, and clothes.*

◀ *The male Goliath beetle of Africa is the world's heaviest insect. It can be more than 40 in. (110 mm) long and weigh 3.5 oz. (100 g).*

▼ *Ladybugs are helpful predators, as both larvae and adults kill aphids. Many beetles are pests, eating crops or trees.*

Ladybug

▼ *Houseflies will eat fresh or rotting food, and often lay their eggs in dung.*

Housefly

◀ *To escape their enemies, some insects have developed clever camouflages. The cryptic mantid can escape predators because of its close resemblance to a leaf. Other insects are mimics, with similar coloring to a distasteful or dangerous insect.*

◀ *The Western pygmy blue is one of the smallest butterflies.*

PESTS AND PARASITES
Insects such as mosquitoes spread disease; other pests eat crops and human food. Parasitic wasps paralyze and lay eggs on their prey, which then feeds the wasp larvae.

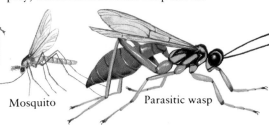

Cockroach

Mosquito

Parasitic wasp

SOCIAL INSECTS
Social insects, such as ants, function only as colony members. The colony's activities center on the egg-laying queen. Most of her eggs hatch into female workers or soldiers. Males exist solely to fertilize new queens, after which they die. Some wasps and bees are also social insects.

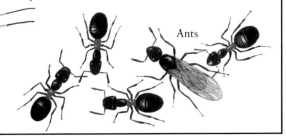

Ants

Fish

The first fish appeared in the oceans some 540 million years ago. By breathing through gills, fish have always been fully adapted to life in water. About 60 percent of all fish species live in salt water; a few kinds can live in either salt or fresh water. There are three main groups of fish: Agnatha or jawless fish (lampreys and hagfish), Chondrichthyes or fish with a skeleton of cartilage (sharks, chimaeras, and rays), and Osteichthyes, a group that includes some 20,000 species of fish with a bony skeleton.

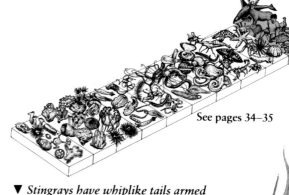

See pages 34–35

FISH RECORDS

- The biggest freshwater fish is the giant catfish, at 16 ft. (5 m) long (a record set in the 1800s).
- The longest bony fish is the oarfish, up to 50 ft. (15 m) long.
- The smallest fish is the dwarf goby of the Pacific Ocean. Few grow more than 0.3 in. (9 mm) long.
- Largest of all fish is the whale shark: 60 ft. (18 m) long and weighing 15 tons.

Whale shark

- Coelacanths live deep in the Indian Ocean. Scientists believed they had died out 70 million years ago—until one was caught in 1938.
- Fish known to attack people include some sharks (whites, blues, hammerheads), barracudas, and moray eels. Venomous fish include stonefish, with poisonous spines.

Coelacanth

HOW FISH BREATHE

Fish breathe oxygen from water by means of gills; water contains amounts of dissolved oxygen. The fish gulps in water through its mouth. The water passes across the gills and out again. Blood flows through the gills in tiny filters that take oxygen in, and release waste carbon dioxide.

Water out

Water in through mouth

Gill bars

Blood capillaries

Filaments

Filaments

Direction of water flow

Deoxygenated blood pumped to gills

▼ Stingrays have whiplike tails armed with poisonous spines. They are ocean bottom-dwellers with flattened bodies.

Stingray

▶ A mako shark, is about 11 ft. (3.5 m) long. Makos prey on fish but sometimes attack human bathers and small boats.

Mako shark

▼ The alligator gar is a large 10 ft. (3 m) freshwater hunter of North America. It has an alligatorlike snout.

▼ The saltwater herring is an important North Atlantic food fish. Members of the herring family include shad and sardine.

Alligator gar

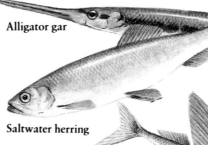

Saltwater herring

▶ Flying fish glide rather than fly. To escape predators they take off, using their long pectoral fins as wings.

Flying fish

JAWLESS FISH
Lampreys and hagfish lack true jaws, but have sucking mouths with horny teeth. They clamp onto a victim and tear its flesh with file-toothed tongues.

Lamprey

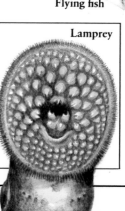

▶ *Puffer fish keep away their enemies by doubling their size; by quickly taking in water or air they inflate their stomachs.*

Puffer fish

▼ *Chub are freshwater fish related to carp. Like most jawed fish, they have scales.*

Chub

Seahorse

African cichlid

PARENTHOOD
Only a few fish protect their young. Some cichlids shelter their young in their mouths. Baby seahorses hatch and develop in a pouch on their father's body.

Butterfly fish

◀ *Tropical coral reefs shelter great numbers of brightly colored fish, like this long-nosed butterfly fish.*

▲ *The cleaner wrasse eats parasites from the skin of larger fish.*

▼ *Tuna or are large, fast fish that are good to eat. A bluefin tuna can weigh 2,000 pounds (900 kg).*

Eel

▶ *Eels have long, snake-like bodies. Some eels, such as the European eel and American eel, migrate from rivers to the oceans in order to spawn. Other eels, like the fierce moray eel, live only in the sea.*

Catfish

Bluefin tuna

Anglerfish

▲ *Catfish are ocean bottom-feeders, using their whiskerlike barbels to feel in mud.*

▲ *The anglerfish has on its head rodlike growths with a fleshy tip. This wormlike "bait" lures smaller fish within snapping range of its jaws.*

A FISH OUT OF WATER
Lungfish breathe through air bladders as well as gills. During a drought the fish survives by burying itself in the mud, motionless and barely breathing, until the rains come.

Lungfish

Burrow

Amphibians

Amphibians are a relatively small group of coldblooded vertebrate animals: about 3,000 species. Many are water creatures. Others live on land, in trees, and even in deserts. Most amphibians need water (a river, pond, or even a droplet on a leaf) to lay their eggs. There are three orders: wormlike caecilians (Apoda); newts and salamanders (Urodela), with long tails and usually four legs; and toads and frogs (Anura), tailless and four-legged. Amphibians are most common in warm climates.

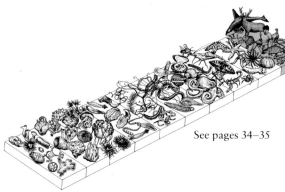

See pages 34–35

LIFE CYCLE OF A FROG

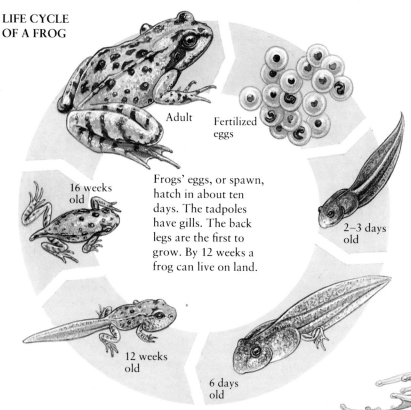

Adult

Fertilized eggs

Frogs' eggs, or spawn, hatch in about ten days. The tadpoles have gills. The back legs are the first to grow. By 12 weeks a frog can live on land.

2–3 days old

16 weeks old

12 weeks old

6 days old

▶ *Most amphibians simply deposit their spawn and leave the young to fend for themselves. But some make nests in leaves or burrows, or even out of a special foam. A few carry their offspring around with them, or even hide them in their mouths. Baby Surinam toads emerge from eggs encased in pockets of their mother's skin. The male midwife toad attaches its eggs to its hind legs and carries them for about three weeks until they hatch.*

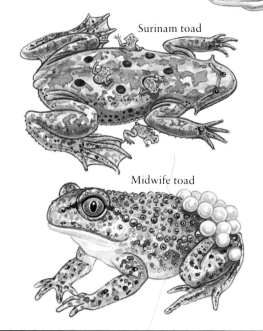

Surinam toad

Midwife toad

HOW DO FROGS AND TOADS DIFFER?

Frogs spend more time in water than toads, which can live in drier places.

Frog skin is smooth, toad skin is lumpy.

Frogs use their long legs for jumping. Toads crawl.

Frogs have moist skin, toads have dry skin.

▲ *Frogs and toads are the largest order of amphibians, with some 2,700 species. They are very diverse in their habitats. Some, like the spadefoots, burrow in the ground; others spend almost all their time in water. Some have disklike pads on their toes for climbing. There is even a species (Rattray's frog) whose tadpoles drown in water.*

WHY DO FROGS AND TOADS CROAK?

Male frogs croak to call females during the mating season by forcing air over their vocal chords. In some species, females also call, but less loudly. The loudest croakers are species with an expanding vocal sac.

Tree frog

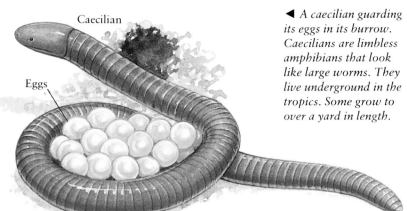

Caecilian

Eggs

◀ *A caecilian guarding its eggs in its burrow. Caecilians are limbless amphibians that look like large worms. They live underground in the tropics. Some grow to over a yard in length.*

◀ *A toad capturing a meal with its long, sticky-tipped tongue.* Most frogs and toads eat insects and other small animals. They usually hunt by staying still and aiming precisely at their target. Some frogs have teeth.

▲ *The Mexican axolotl is an amphibian that never grows up. This newtlike creature spends its life in water, breathing by means of gills. Only in unusual conditions does it develop lungs. The axolotl usually breeds in its gilled state.*

Eft

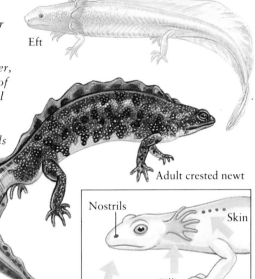

Adult crested newt

Nostrils

Skin

Mouth

Gills

Common frog

FACTS ABOUT AMPHIBIANS

Golden poison-dart frog

● The largest amphibian is the giant salamander of China, 3 ft. (1 m) long and weighing up to 66 pounds (30 kg).
● The smallest amphibian is the Cuban frog, *Sminthillus limbatus*, less than half an inch (12 mm) long.
● One Colombian golden poison-dart frog has enough toxin in its body to kill 1,000 people.
● Mudpuppies, waterdogs, and olms never leave the water.
● The biggest frog is the African goliath frog: it is 3 ft. (88 cm) long and weighs nearly 9 pounds (4 kg).
● There is no truth in the legend that a salamander can pass through fire unhurt.

COURTSHIP

Not all amphibians mate in water. Courtship takes place in spring, and is often a frenzied affair. Males and females make their way to suitable breeding locations and large numbers may congregate to mate. The male long-tailed salamander indulges in an energetic display; dancing and grappling with the female to persuade her to accept a small packet of his sperm. The eggs are fertilized inside the female's body.

Long-tailed salamanders

HOW AMPHIBIANS BREATHE

Amphibians breathe by taking air into their lungs, but they also breathe in air through the skin, mouth, and throat. A young newt or frog starts its life as a tadpole with gills, but develops lungs as it matures and is able to leave the water. Newts, also called efts (see above), are very like salamanders, but are more aquatic.

Fire salamander

Reptiles

There are more than 6,500 species of reptiles: some 250 kinds of tortoises and turtles (order Testudinidae); 25 species of crocodiles and alligators (order Crocodilia); about 2,800 species of snakes (order Squamata); 3,700 species of lizards (order Squamata); and the unique tuatara (order Rhynchocephalia). Like amphibians, reptiles are cold blooded. Most live in the tropics, though a few snakes and lizards live in cooler climates. Reptiles have scaly skins and most lay leathery-shelled eggs.

See pages 34–35

SNAKES

▶ *Poisonous snakes bite with grooved fangs which inject venom from saclike glands in the head. Many venomous snakes are brightly colored as a warning.*

Coral snake

Cobra

Venom sac

Fang

◀ *Male rattlesnakes wrestle for mates, but do not use their poison fangs. The rattle is formed by horny plates at the tip of the tail. Rattlesnakes detect prey with heat-sensing organs.*

▲ *Vipers, which include copperheads and rattlesnakes, have long fangs that unfold from the roof of the mouth as the snake strikes. Cobras and sea snakes have short, fixed fangs. Poisonous snakes can bite as soon as they have hatched.*

◀ *Snakes can swallow objects larger than their heads. The egg-eating snake swallows the egg, then crushes the shell.*

LIZARDS

▶ *The little gecko has suckerlike pads on its feet. It can run across the ceiling of a room with ease when hunting insects.*

▲ *The Gila monster is a poisonous lizard from the southwestern United States. Like all coldblooded animals, this desert-dweller is most active when warmed by the sun; its body is as warm or as cool as its surroundings.*

◀ *The chameleon's color changes are the result of hormone activity triggered by a change of light or temperature, or by fear or anger. Chameleons catch insects by shooting out their long, sticky tongues.*

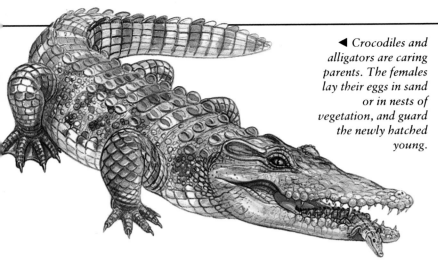

◄ Crocodiles and alligators are caring parents. The females lay their eggs in sand or in nests of vegetation, and guard the newly hatched young.

FACTS ABOUT REPTILES

Aldabra giant tortoise

- Largest lizard: Komodo dragon (a monitor lizard) of Indonesia, 10 ft. (3 m) long.
- Largest snakes: anaconda (South America) and reticulated python (Asia): up to 30 ft. (9 m).
- Largest crocodile: estuarine crocodile of Southeast Asia: up to 23 ft. (7 m) long.
- Heaviest turtle: leatherback, about 6.5 ft. (2 m) long and wide, and weighing over 1,000 pounds (450 kg).
- There are two species of giant tortoise, one living on the Seychelles and Aldabra islands, the other on the Galápagos Islands.
- The slowworm looks like a snake, but is actually a lizard that has lost its limbs.
- There are other legless lizards, such as the glass snake and amphisbaena.

CROCODILES AND THEIR RELATIVES

Crocodiles, alligators, caimans, and gavials are large carnivores with strong jaws and powerful tails. They either bask on river banks or lie almost submerged in the water with only their eyes, nostrils, and ears showing. The crocodile's fourth tooth sticks out when its jaws are shut: in the broader-headed alligator this tooth is hidden. Gavials, or gharials, have long, thin snouts.

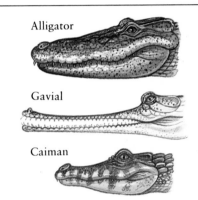

Alligator

Gavial

Caiman

◄ Like pythons and boas, anacondas are constrictors—they kill their prey by squeezing and suffocating it.

Anaconda

TURTLES AND TORTOISES

Turtles and tortoises are reptiles with shells. Only the head, legs, and tail stick out. The name tortoise is often used for land-living Testudinidae. Marine turtles are excellent swimmers. So are freshwater terrapins. Turtles and tortoises prefer warm climates. Some are plant-eaters, while others are carnivorous.

► Sea turtles come ashore to lay their eggs in sand. The hatchlings scramble out and race for the safety of the water. Only a few escape the waiting predators.

Marine turtle

Birds

Some prehistoric reptiles jumped or glided from tree to tree and, over millions of years, reptile scales became feathers. Birds are the only animals with feathers—they keep a bird warm, even in sub-zero temperatures, and they make flight possible. There are 28 orders and about 8,600 species of birds. These include water birds (wildfowl, waders, and seabirds), birds of prey (eagles, hawks, and owls), and "passerine" or perching birds, most of which live among trees or other high places when not flying.

See pages 34–35

THE 28 ORDERS OF THE CLASS AVES (BIRDS)

1 Struthioniformes: large, flightless birds, one species survives; ostrich.

2 Rheiformes: two species of flightless birds of South America; rhea.

3 Casuariiformes: large flightless birds of Australia, New Guinea; cassowary, emu.

4 Apterygiformes: nocturnal, flightless birds of New Zealand; kiwi.

5 Tinamiformes: weak-flying ground birds of S. and C. America; tinamou.

6 Sphenisciformes: flightless swimming birds with erect posture; penguin.

7 Gaviiformes: web-footed diving birds of Asia, America, Europe; diver, loon.

8 Podicipediformes: diving birds with long toes with flaplike lobes; grebe.

9 Procellariiformes: ocean birds with tubelike noses; petrel, shearwater, albatross.

10 Pelecaniformes: fully webbed feet, beak, pouch; pelican, cormorant, gannet.

11 Ciconiiformes: long-legged waders; heron, egret, stork, spoonbill, ibis.

12 Anseriformes: water birds; duck, goose, swan, screamer.

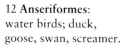

17 Pintailed sandgrouse

19 Macaw

22 Whippoorwill

28 Eurasian robin

20 Yellow-billed cuckoo

15 Black crowned crane

2 Rhea

12 Black swan

10 Pelican

16 Caspian tern

4 Kiwi

13 Bald eagle

13 Falconiformes: birds of prey; eagle, buzzard, hawk, falcon, vulture.

14 Galliformes: fowl-like birds; quail, chicken, peacock, pheasant, turkey.

15 Gruiformes: marsh and land birds; rail, crane, coot, moorhen, bustard, trumpeter.

16 Charadriiformes: waders and water-birds; gull, sandpiper, plover, curlew, tern, oystercatcher, auk.

17 Pteroclidiformes: medium-sized birds with long, pointed wings; sandgrouse.

18 Columbiformes: medium-sized short-legged birds; pigeons, doves.

19 Psittaciformes: seed- and fruit-eaters with grasping claws; parrots, lories, cockatoos.

20 Cuculiformes: tree and ground-dwelling; cuckoo, touraco, roadrunner.

21 Strigiformes: mostly nighttime silent birds of prey with large heads; owl.

22 Caprimulgiformes: nighttime insect-eaters; nightjar, oilbird, frogmouth.

23 Apodiformes: weak-footed, strong wings, spend most of their lives flying; swift, hummingbird.

24 Trogoniformes: long-tailed forest birds with small, weak feet; trogon.

25 Coliiformes: small, long-tailed African fruit-eaters with four toes; coly, mousebird.

26 Coraciiformes: long bills, short legs; kingfisher, bee-eater, roller, hoopoe.

27 Piciformes: woodland birds that nest in holes; toucan, woodpecker, barbet.

28 Passeriformes: 60 families, over 5,000 species; broadbills, all songbirds (crow, lark, finch, thrush, etc.).

23 Alpine swift

24 Resplendent quetzal

1 Ostrich

18 Turtledove

9 Shearwater

25 Mousebird

3 Emu

26 Kingfisher

21 Barn owl

27 Toco toucan

11 Great blue heron

6 Adélie penguin

14 Lady Amherst's pheasant

8 Great crested grebe

5 Tinamou

7 Red-throated diver

49

Bird Behavior

To call someone "bird-brained" should be a compliment, for bird behavior is amazingly complex, a mixture of learned skills—such as a pigeon getting food from a bird feeder—and instinct, as in the territorial aggression of a European robin. Flight enables birds to be extraordinary travelers and some species migrate across oceans and continents. Finding food in all kinds of habitats, mating, and nest-building, birds around the world demonstrate a remarkable range of adaptations and techniques.

Osprey

Corn bunting

Teal

▶ *Depending on its species, a bird has between 940 and 25,000 feathers. In most species, the male has more colorful feathers than the female.*

Siberian jay

BIRDS' FEET
Most birds have four, clawed toes, adapted to suit different ways of life. Perching birds (for example, the corn bunting) have three forward-pointing toes and one backward-pointing one. Ducks have webbed feet, for swimming. The osprey's talons seize and crush prey.

FEATHERS
Feathers are replaced (molted) once or twice a year. A flight feather (*right*) has a central rod or quill. In close-up, the threadlike barbs can be seen; these are held together by smaller hooked fibers called barbules.

Barbule

Quill

WING SHAPES
Long, slender wings like those of the albatross are best for effortless, gliding flight. Fast fliers, such as hawks, have narrow, pointed wings. Game birds like the partridge have stubby wings; good for quick takeoffs and brief dashes.

Albatross

Hobby

Partridge

BIRDS' BILLS
Many water birds use their bills as probes or sieves. Woodpeckers' bills are wood drills. Seed- and nut-eaters have bills for cracking hard outer shells. Birds of prey have hooked bills for tearing flesh.

Woodpecker (drill)

Crossbill (nutcracker)

Kestrel (tearing)

Spoonbill (detector/sieve)

Oystercatcher (probe)

NESTS

Some birds, such as the plover, lay eggs in a scrape on the ground among sand or stones. Water birds, such as grebes, nest on or beside the water. Swallows are mud-builders, often nesting against walls of buildings. Many songbirds, such as the thrush, nest in trees or bushes, building a nest from twigs, leaves, and grass in which to lay their eggs.

Plover's scrape

Grebe's nest

Swallow's nest

Robin's nest

FACTS ABOUT BIRDS

- The ostrich is the biggest bird, 9 ft. (2.7 m) tall, weighing 340 pounds (156 kg), and lays the biggest egg, weighing about 4 pounds (1.7 kg).
- The smallest bird is the bee hummingbird of Cuba, less than 2 inches (5 cm) long and weighing only 0.05 oz. (1.6 grams).
- The wandering albatross has the biggest wingspan: over 10 ft. (3 m).
- Bird song is a signal, usually telling other birds to stay off the singer's territory. Parents and chicks can recognize each other's voices.
- The peregrine falcon is credited with a top diving speed of more than 180 mph (300 km/h).

▼ *Eider ducks are valued for the soft down on their breasts, used in bedding; they are also one of the world's fastest flying birds.*

COURTSHIP

Many birds have elaborate courtship behavior, in which males dance or display colorful plumage to attract females. The Australian lyrebird has long tail feathers which it displays during its courtship.

Lyrebird

MIGRATION

Many birds make amazingly long migrations. Different species may be seen in flight along favored routes, often in large flocks. The Arctic tern makes the longest migratory journey of any animal. It flies up to 22,000 miles (36,000 km) in a year, journeying south from its Arctic breeding grounds to the Antarctic summer, and back again.

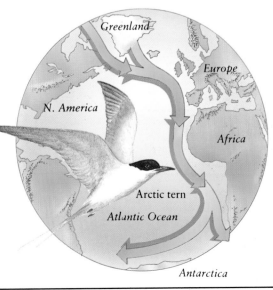

Greenland

Europe

N. America

Africa

Arctic tern

Atlantic Ocean

Antarctica

Mammals

Mammals are one of the eight classes of vertebrate (backboned) animals. There are far fewer species of mammals than other groups of animals—but mammals have adapted to a wider range of habitats. Mammals live on land, in hot or cold climates, in the sea, and have even taken to the air. Mammals feed their young on the mother's milk, they protect their young, they have hair, they maintain a constant body temperature, and they have relatively larger brains than other animals.

See pages 34–35

16 Dugong

14 African elephant

8 Pangolin

2 Koala

11 Dolphin

15 Hyrax

12 Lion

1 Echidna

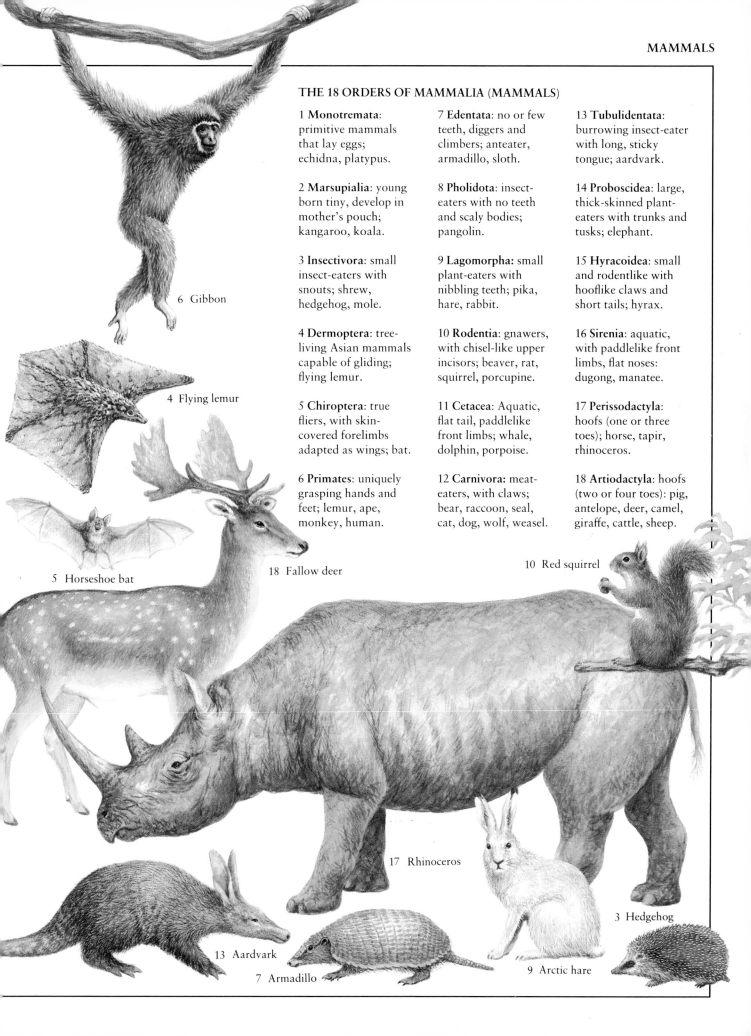

THE 18 ORDERS OF MAMMALIA (MAMMALS)

1 Monotremata: primitive mammals that lay eggs; echidna, platypus.

2 Marsupialia: young born tiny, develop in mother's pouch; kangaroo, koala.

3 Insectivora: small insect-eaters with snouts; shrew, hedgehog, mole.

4 Dermoptera: tree-living Asian mammals capable of gliding; flying lemur.

5 Chiroptera: true fliers, with skin-covered forelimbs adapted as wings; bat.

6 Primates: uniquely grasping hands and feet; lemur, ape, monkey, human.

7 Edentata: no or few teeth, diggers and climbers; anteater, armadillo, sloth.

8 Pholidota: insect-eaters with no teeth and scaly bodies; pangolin.

9 Lagomorpha: small plant-eaters with nibbling teeth; pika, hare, rabbit.

10 Rodentia: gnawers, with chisel-like upper incisors; beaver, rat, squirrel, porcupine.

11 Cetacea: Aquatic, flat tail, paddlelike front limbs; whale, dolphin, porpoise.

12 Carnivora: meat-eaters, with claws; bear, raccoon, seal, cat, dog, wolf, weasel.

13 Tubulidentata: burrowing insect-eater with long, sticky tongue; aardvark.

14 Proboscidea: large, thick-skinned plant-eaters with trunks and tusks; elephant.

15 Hyracoidea: small and rodentlike with hooflike claws and short tails; hyrax.

16 Sirenia: aquatic, with paddlelike front limbs, flat noses; dugong, manatee.

17 Perissodactyla: hoofs (one or three toes); horse, tapir, rhinoceros.

18 Artiodactyla: hoofs (two or four toes): pig, antelope, deer, camel, giraffe, cattle, sheep.

6 Gibbon

4 Flying lemur

5 Horseshoe bat

18 Fallow deer

10 Red squirrel

17 Rhinoceros

13 Aardvark

7 Armadillo

9 Arctic hare

3 Hedgehog

Mammal Senses

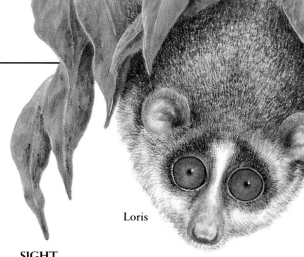

Mammals are constantly receiving messages from their senses, on which their next meal or their lives may depend. Many mammals have senses far more acute than our own: keener eyesight and hearing, for example, as well as others (like the bat's sonar or the mole's sensitive whiskers) which we simply do not need. The variations in mammal body design are the result of millions of years of evolution and adaptation. So too is mammal behavior, either as individuals or in cooperating groups.

Loris

ANATOMY OF A MAMMAL
SKELETON OF A HORSE

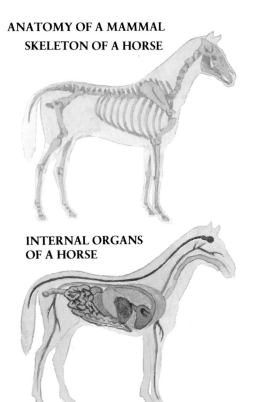

◀ *The skeleton of a mammal acts as a framework for its body and protects vital organs such as the heart and stomach; also, the muscles that enable it to move are attached to its skeleton. An adult mammal—whether a mouse or an elephant—has over 200 bones.*

INTERNAL ORGANS OF A HORSE

◀ *The main internal body systems of a mammal, such as a horse, are concerned with digestion and waste disposal, and reproduction. The skull protects the brain and houses important sense organs such as the eyes, ears, nose, and mouth, linked to the nervous system.*

SIGHT
In most mammals the two eyes are set either side of the head. So each eye gives a different image. A few have binocular vision, with the eyes set in the front of the head and able to work together to focus on one image. This enables the mammal to judge distance more accurately—an important aid for tree climbers, like the loris (a primate), and for hunters, such as cats.

Wild dogs

HIBERNATION
Some species of mammals hibernate: they sleep through all or part of the cold winter when food is scarce. Before hibernating, the animal stores fat in its body. It becomes chilled and its heartbeat slows. A hibernating dormouse will not wake up even if it is touched. Other animals, such as squirrels and badgers, emerge in mild weather to seek food.

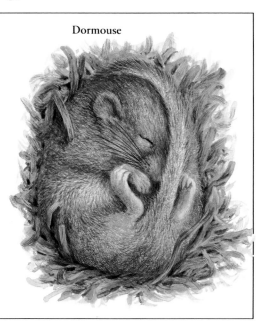

Dormouse

TOUCH
In many mammals the sense of touch is highly developed. They use sensitive hairs or whiskers and inquisitive snouts to investigate their surroundings when either burrowing underground or moving about in darkness. Moles have weak eyes, but rely on touch and smell to find their way through their tunnels.

Mole

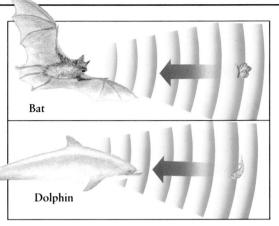

Bat

Dolphin

TASTE
Taste is situated in the tastebuds of the tongue. A dog has about 8,000, a cow four times as many. Anteaters use their long tongues to raid ants' nests.

Anteater

HEARING
Some animals can hear much better than people. Bats in flight and dolphins swimming send out sound waves to detect prey by echolocation. The bat's sonar makes it an aerobatic flier even in the dark, though its eyesight is poor.

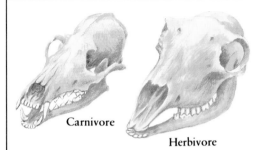

Carnivore

Herbivore

TEETH
Almost all mammals have teeth. Carnivores have sharp incisors and canines for tearing flesh. Herbivores nibble with their front teeth and use grinding molars to crush fibers.

▼ *Carnivores kill for food, but some also feed on dead animals, that they have seen or scented.*

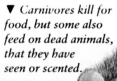

Hyena

Vulture

SMELL AND SCENT
Smell is an important sense for many mammals. Some deposit scent-messages to mark territory. Hunting animals, especially dogs (wild dogs, wolves, and foxes), track prey by smell. Hunting lions approach a herd of zebras from downwind, so that their smell is not carried toward the prey, alerting them to the danger.

ANIMAL INTELLIGENCE
Chimpanzees are the most intelligent apes. Inquisitive and persevering, they will imitate human actions and can solve simple problems. Only dolphins rival chimps in intelligence. Rats, dogs, and pigs also perform well in animal intelligence tests.

Chimpanzee

Rat

Dog

Pig

Dolphin

Animal Homes

Most animals need homes only to shelter their young. Birds build nests, a female bear seeks a den, a vixen (a female fox) takes over a burrow. Some social animals live in large colonies, used for many generations. The colony's home may be a structure of remarkable size—like a prairie dog town or a termite nest. Most hunting and grazing animals have no fixed homes, but wander their territories in search of food. Each individual or group may fiercely defend its territory against rivals of the same species.

◀ *The water spider is the only spider that can live under water. It builds a "diving bell" of silk which it fills with bubbles of air carried down from the surface. Inside the air-filled bell, the spider lives, mates, and lays its eggs.*

◀ *Carmine bee-eaters, African birds related to kingfishers, nest in holes in river banks. The nest protects the young until they are old enough to fly. Birds' nests vary from complex woven or mud structures to holes or simple scrapes in the ground.*

▶ *Most bats are active at night. By day they shelter in caves, trees, or the roofs or cellars of buildings. Large numbers may roost together, hanging upside down by their feet and huddled close for warmth.*

A BEAVER'S LODGE
Beavers build island homes in rivers. They use chisel-like teeth and strong claws to build a log dam. The dam creates a pond in which they build a lodge, a mound of sticks and mud with dry inner chambers and underwater entrances.

PRAIRIE DOG TOWN

Prairie dogs are burrowing rodents of the grasslands of North America. Hundreds may live together in a colony or town. Family groups dig territorial burrows as deep as 16 ft. (5 m). Sentries keep watch above ground for predators.

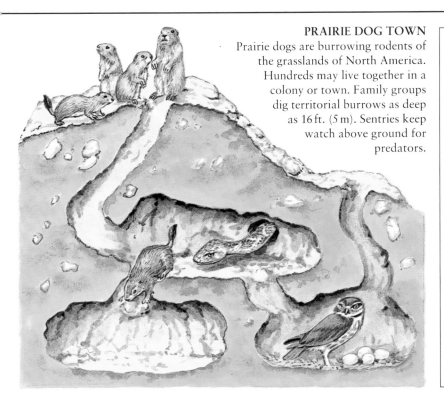

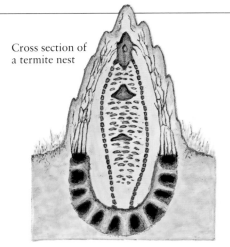

Cross section of a termite nest

TERMITE NEST

Termites have the most amazing homes; these social insects build mud mounds 30 ft. (9 m) high. Some termite nests have sloping roofs to deflect rain. Australian compass termites align their narrow nests north-south to escape too much hot sun.

TERRITORY

Many animals are territorial. They will fight rivals for an area that is big enough to provide its occupants with food, breeding space, and shelter. Territorial limits are respected. A rabbit will retreat, even when being chased, if it reaches a territorial "no-go" zone.

SAFETY IN NUMBERS

Many grazers and browsers (cattle, sheep, deer, antelope, horses) live in herds, sometimes hundreds strong. Deer form groups of females and young, each led by a strong male. Herd living has advantages. Every animal is a lookout, alert for danger. The strongest animals will often defend the herd. Females may help one another with young. By being one of a crowd, an individual has a smaller chance of being singled out for attack by predators and more chance of escaping in the confusion as the herd runs away.

Animal Movement

All animals move at some time in their lives—even the limpet clinging to its rock began life as a free-swimming juvenile. Fast movement is essential for many animals, to hunt and to escape when hunted. To conserve energy, fast-moving animals usually sprint only when they have to, in bursts. Some have no need of speed, relying on other strategies such as camouflage or armor for protection. Other animals are marathon athletes, traveling immense distances during seasonal migrations.

ANIMALS ON LAND
Legs act like props and levers. In motion, the legs push against the ground, propeling the animals forward.

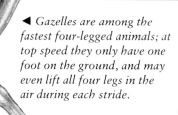

◄ *Gazelles are among the fastest four-legged animals; at top speed they only have one foot on the ground, and may even lift all four legs in the air during each stride.*

◄ *Arachnids (spiders and scorpions) have eight legs that move rather like the oars in a rowboat.*

▼ *Squids and octopuses swim by taking water in and then squirting it out through a tube; the expelled water causes them to shoot backward.*

Water in

WITHOUT LEGS
Not all animals need legs to move quickly. The fastest snake, the black mamba, can reach over 18 mph (30 km/h). Many snakes move with a wriggling motion *(top)*. Burrowing snakes move in accordianlike contractions *(below)*.

▼ *Snails and slugs have a single foot used for clinging and motion. The animal moves in rhythmic muscular waves by extending and withdrawing its foot. Slime helps the snail move, and leaves the familiar glistening trail.*

ANIMAL SPEEDS
Animal speeds are difficult to measure accurately. The fastest fish, the sailfin, narrowly outsprints the fastest land animal, the cheetah. But in flight, an eider duck in level flight would be overtaken by a diving peregrine falcon.

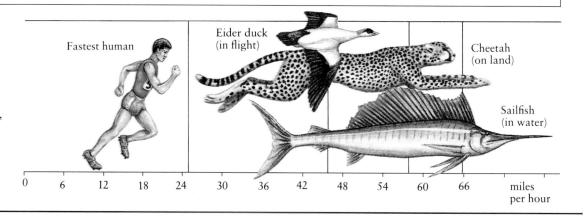

Fastest human

Eider duck (in flight)

Cheetah (on land)

Sailfish (in water)

| 0 | 6 | 12 | 18 | 24 | 30 | 36 | 42 | 48 | 54 | 60 | 66 | miles per hour |

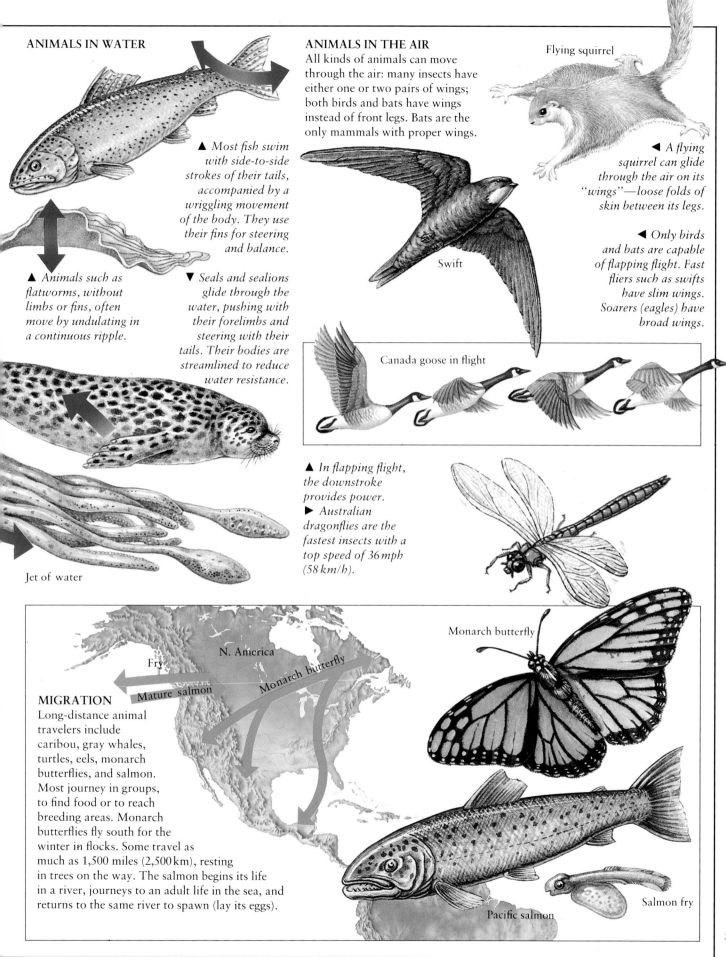

ANIMALS IN WATER

▲ Most fish swim with side-to-side strokes of their tails, accompanied by a wriggling movement of the body. They use their fins for steering and balance.

▲ Animals such as flatworms, without limbs or fins, often move by undulating in a continuous ripple.

▼ Seals and sealions glide through the water, pushing with their forelimbs and steering with their tails. Their bodies are streamlined to reduce water resistance.

Jet of water

ANIMALS IN THE AIR

All kinds of animals can move through the air: many insects have either one or two pairs of wings; both birds and bats have wings instead of front legs. Bats are the only mammals with proper wings.

Flying squirrel

◄ A flying squirrel can glide through the air on its "wings"—loose folds of skin between its legs.

◄ Only birds and bats are capable of flapping flight. Fast fliers such as swifts have slim wings. Soarers (eagles) have broad wings.

Swift

Canada goose in flight

▲ In flapping flight, the downstroke provides power.
► Australian dragonflies are the fastest insects with a top speed of 36 mph (58 km/h).

Monarch butterfly

MIGRATION

Long-distance animal travelers include caribou, gray whales, turtles, eels, monarch butterflies, and salmon. Most journey in groups, to find food or to reach breeding areas. Monarch butterflies fly south for the winter in flocks. Some travel as much as 1,500 miles (2,500 km), resting in trees on the way. The salmon begins its life in a river, journeys to an adult life in the sea, and returns to the same river to spawn (lay its eggs).

Fry

N. America

Mature salmon

Monarch butterfly

Pacific salmon

Salmon fry

Animals and their Young

An animal's life span is determined chiefly by the time it needs to reproduce. Wild animals face many hazards and few survive to extreme old age. Most records for longevity have been set by captive animals. Reproduction in animals takes two forms: asexual, when only one parent produces the young (such as budding in sponges or corals), and sexual (when male and female sex cells combine to form a new animal). Some animals can regenerate parts of their bodies; for example, a crab can grow a new claw.

LIFESPANS

Turtle

Elephant

Chimpanzee

Starling

Squirrel

Wasp

▲ Animals live much shorter lives than plants. Over 20 is old for most mammals. The potential lifespan of animals ranges from over 60 years (elephant, killer whale) to a few weeks or even a single day (adult mayfly).

0   10   20   30   40   50   60   70   80   90   100 yrs

COURTSHIP
Mating involves pairing of males and females. Courtship rituals often involve elaborate behavior, especially in birds. Egrets grow long plumes during the mating season and display these feathers as part of their courtship dance. Some animals pair for life, others mate and then part.

LIVING TOGETHER
Mammal babies take months or even years to develop. A female bear, by nature a solitary hunter, guards her young with care and teaches the cubs to catch fish. Bears are carnivores, but they also eat other kinds of food including grubs, birds' eggs, and berries. The cubs are energetic and playful: through play they learn the skills necessary to survive. Usually the cubs will stay with their mother for one or two years.

— Males follow behind

▶ Elephants are sociable animals. They move in herds, feeding as they go. The herd is led by a dominant older female. A female giving birth is watched over by other female "midwives." If one elephant is trapped or wounded, other herd members will come to its aid.

Dominant female elephant (matriarch) leads herd

▲ Male elephants (bulls) usually stay behind the herd. Rogues are aggressive males that live apart from a herd.

MAMMAL REPRODUCTION
Placental mammals

Most mammal species have a placenta, a two-way filter that joins the unborn baby to its mother's body. Through it the baby gets food and oxygen from the mother's blood. After birth, the mother suckles it on her milk.

Red kangaroo

Monotremes

These are the most primitive mammals, found only in Australia and New Guinea. The female lays eggs, but when the young hatch they are fed on milk from her body.

Zebra with foal

Marsupials

Pouched mammals, or marsupials, give birth to live young, but the young are born only partially developed. The tiny baby crawls into a pouch on its mother's body. Inside the pouch, it feeds on milk from her body, and will return to the pouch for shelter even when big enough to emerge.

Duckbilled platypus

LOOKING AFTER THE YOUNG

King penguin

Trout

◄ A male king penguin of the Antarctic keeps its egg warm beneath a flap of skin on its feet. The chick is sheltered in the same place.

▲ Fish, with few exceptions, simply deposit their eggs and swim away. The young that hatch must look after themselves.

GESTATION PERIODS

Gestation is the time between fertilization and birth. Incubation is the time between fertilization and the hatching of an egg. A female elephant's pregnancy lasts 20 to 22 months. A fruit fly takes less than a day to change from egg to larva.

```
0   0.25  0.5  0.75  1.0  1.25  1.5  1.75  2.0
                                         years
```

Giraffe
Elephant
Gibbon
Lion
Dog
Rabbit

► Many baby mammals are born hairless, blind, and helpless. Fox cubs are dependent on their mother for warmth and food for the first weeks of life.

Fox with cubs

Macaque

◄ Parents teach by example. Many animals have complex behavior patterns which the young inherit. Monkeys, for example, exhibit learned skills—such as specialized food-gathering techniques. By watching its mother, this baby macaque learns to copy her behavior.

FACTS ABOUT ANIMAL LIVES

- The longest-lived sea creature is the quahog clam (150 years).
- A queen ant may live for 18 years, some spiders for as long as 25 years.
- A mayfly emerges from the larval stage, breeds, and dies in a few hours.
- Sturgeon (80) and carp (50) are among the longest-lived fish.
- Record litters are 19 (cat), 23 (dog), 34 (mouse). These records were all set by pet animals.

Mayfly

Animals and People

People first hunted animals, then domesticated some species for food or wool, or as beasts of burden. Today domestic animals still carry goods and provide us with food, textiles, and other materials. Through selective breeding people have changed animals. The growth of population has destroyed many animal habitats. Wild animals live alongside people in town and country. Some thrive (pigeons, cockroaches, rats, fleas). Many others face an uncertain future, possibly extinction.

ANIMALS THAT ARE USEFUL TO PEOPLE

▲ *One of the most unusual animal providers is the silkmoth larva, which produces a cocoon from which natural silk is obtained. One type of silkworm is raised on silk farms; wild silk comes from silkworms living wild in China and India.*

DAIRY FOODS
Milk, butter, yogurt, cheese: from cows, sheep, horses, goats, reindeer, and camels.

MEAT AND FISH
Beef (cattle), pork and bacon (pigs), lamb and mutton (sheep), goat, poultry, fish.

LEATHER
Hides from cattle, sheep, goats, even farmed alligators, for making leather.

TEXTILES
Wool from sheep, goats, camels, llamas. Silk from silkworm. Down from ducks.

LOAD CARRIERS
The dog was probably the first domestic animal. Native Americans used dogs as pack animals. Over 5,000 years ago horses, asses, and camels were tamed for riding and for carrying loads. Oxen pulled heavy plows and carts.

Camel

Horse

Donkey

◄ *The animals that are most useful to people provide fur, skin, or wool as well as meat and milk; they include sheep, cattle, llamas, and camels. Other animals are useful because they can help people to hunt or get around, while some animals can carry loads or messages.*

ANIMAL COMPANIONS

The first pets were probably baby animals (wolf cubs, goat kids, birds) brought back by prehistoric hunters for children to play with. For thousands of years, and in every society, people have valued animals as companions. To the lonely and elderly a dog or cat can be both a friend and a comfort; pets can sometimes have a beneficial effect on people who are ill.

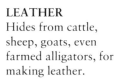

◄ *People have kept dogs as pets and helpers since prehistoric times. No dog is more valued than the guide dog, trained as the "eyes" of its blind or partially sighted human owner.*

► *Bees not only provide us with honey, they also help to pollinate many plants, including fruit trees and garden flowers. People have kept bees for centuries as honey used to be the only sweetener for foods.*

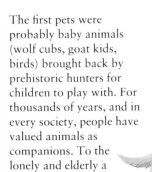

DANGEROUS ANIMALS

Few animals attack people unless provoked and genuine man-eaters are rare. Venomous insects and spiders, and disease-carrying flies are more likely to cause people harm than are sharks, tigers, alligators, or snakes.

Brazilian wandering spider

Great white shark

▲ *The most venomous spider is a species of Brazilian wandering spider. It can hide in clothing or shoes, and give a fatal bite.*

Crocodile

▲ *Sharks have a worse reputation than they deserve, but great whites can be very dangerous.*

▲ *Crocodiles and alligators occasionally attack people, dragging them under the water.*

Tsetse fly

◄ *The tsetse fly feeds on blood and spreads the sleeping sickness, a serious disease.*

◄ *Snapping turtles protect themselves with their strong jaws; these American freshwater turtles can give a painful bite to unwary swimmers.*

Snapping turtle

ANIMALS AS PETS

Favorite pets include hamsters, gerbils, goldfish, birds such as parakeets, parrots, and canaries, rabbits, guinea pigs, cats, and dogs. Only animals bred in captivity should be kept as pets. As a rule, wild animals do not make good pets.

FACTS ABOUT PETS

• The best "talkers" among pet birds are African gray parrots, parakeets, and mynahs.
• Cats usually live longer than dogs. The oldest cat on record lived to be 36.
• Cats kept ancient Egypt's granaries rat-free. People worshiped the cat-goddess Bastet (Bubastis), mourned cats' deaths, and often mummified their bodies.
• Guinea pigs are descendants of wild South American rodents called cavies. Hamsters come from Syria; all pet hamsters are descended from a pair brought to England in 1930.

SELECTIVE BREEDING

The many breeds of dog, from Great Danes to Chihuahuas, share a common wolflike ancestor. Domestic cats are thought to be descended from African wildcats that were originally tamed by the ancient Egyptians. Since the 1800s, the increasing popularity of cats has resulted in much specialist breeding.

▲ *Breeding changed wild horses into strong war horses, the ancestors of the heavy cart and farm horses.*

▼ *A sheepdog obeys the calls of the shepherd as it drives sheep. The dog is carefully trained so that it chases but does not attack the sheep.*

Endangered Animals

Animal species become extinct or die out usually because they cannot adapt to changing conditions. The problem for wildlife today is lack of living space. People compete with wild animals for space, and win. Even prehistoric hunters were efficient enough to wipe out animal populations. The rate of extinctions has accelerated since the 1600s. Many species are in danger; some are being hunted, some are losing their habitat, some are being overrun by other animals, introduced by people.

▲ *Habitat destruction can cause rapid extinction. Forest animals of the tropics are endangered as forests shrink before the chainsaw and bulldozer. Forest monkeys like South America's bearded sakis have only slim chances of survival without protection.*

EXTINCT ANIMALS

Species with no natural enemies are defenseless. The dodo, a flightless pigeon from Mauritius, was extinct by 1680, victim of sailors, cats, and rats who had landed on the island. The great auk was slaughtered for its feathers. The last two were killed in 1844.

VANISHING ANIMALS

Animals close to extinction include the Javan rhino and South China tiger (about 50 left), kakapo of New Zealand (40 or so) and Southeast Asian kouprey or wild ox (about 300). The European bison or wisent, nearly extinct by 1920, survives in Polish reserves.

Dodo

Great auk

European bison

THE SKIN TRADE

Fashion and vanity has brought about the decline of many animal species. Birds such as the egret were hunted for their feathers. Snakes and alligators are killed and skinned to make bags and shoes. The fur trade, though declining, still takes its toll, especially of spotted cats such as the margay.

Margay

Snake

Egret

RIVER POLLUTION

Animals, like people, need clean water. River and lake animals are sensitive to any change in their environment. In the past 50 years farm pesticides, fertilizers, and chemical waste from factories have steadily poisoned many rivers. The European otter *(left)* is no longer seen in most of the rivers where it was once commonly found.

▲ *Even when protected in game reserves, rare animals are not safe from poachers. In Africa, poachers have killed most of the rhinos for their horns. In Indian nature reserves, tigers are poisoned for their skins and bones, which are made into a medicine drunk by Chinese and Koreans.*

◄ *In the 19th century collectors took large numbers of insects, such as butterflies, and birds' eggs for display in their homes. Big game hunters shot animals for trophies, to be similarly displayed. Such activities are frowned on today.*

ZOOS

Since the 1600s the number of human beings has risen from 450 million to over 5 billion. For many people, seeing a bear at the zoo or a lion in a game reserve is the nearest they get to seeing an animal in the wild. Zoos have a role to play in conservation, through education and schemes to save endangered species. However, many people no longer want to stare at lonely animals penned in unsuitable cages.

WOLVES AND PEOPLE

Wolves have survived centuries of persecution, often unjust, by people. These intelligent and adaptable predators were once widespread, as the map shows *(right)*, but now their distribution is greatly reduced. There are now only small numbers of wild wolves in the United States and a few in Europe.

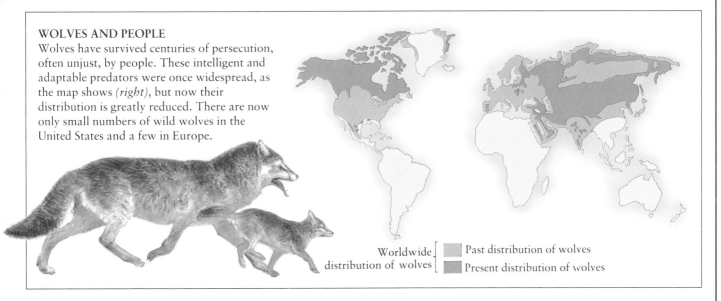

Worldwide distribution of wolves
 ▨ Past distribution of wolves
 ▨ Present distribution of wolves

Prehistoric Animals

Our knowledge of most prehistoric animals comes from their fossil remains, mostly bones and shells. No humans observed the mighty dinosaurs, as the last of these prehistoric reptiles died out 65 million years ago. Prehistoric mammals then became the dominant animals, and from about 4 million years ago mammals such as saber-toothed cats and woolly mammoths shared the Earth with prehistoric humans. By about 10,000 years ago these early mammals had died out or evolved into new species.

BEFORE DINOSAURS
By 350 million years ago, when *Ichthyostega* became the first four-legged animal to invade the land, many types of animals had evolved in the seas; they included early true fish and crustaceans.

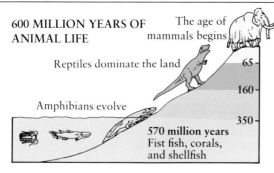

600 MILLION YEARS OF ANIMAL LIFE

The age of mammals begins

Reptiles dominate the land

65 —

160 —

Amphibians evolve

350 —

570 million years Fist fish, corals, and shellfish

Evolution is a natural process of gradual change. Some species are better fitted to life in changing surroundings. They survive. Other, less adaptable species, die out.

DINOSAUR RECORDS
Tallest and heaviest dinosaur: (complete skeleton) *Brachiosaurus*, 72 ft. (22 m), 70 tons; an incomplete skeleton of a *Brachiosaurus*, named *Ultrasaurus*, estimated at 82 ft. (25 m) long and 130 tons.
Longest: *Diplodocus*, almost 88 ft. (27 m) long.
Smallest: chicken-sized *Compsognathus*.
Fiercest carnivore: *Tyrannosaurus rex*, 46 ft. (14 m) long, 12 tons.
Most intelligent?: *Stenonychosaurus* was dog-sized, large-eyed and large-brained.
Most stupid?: *Stegosaurus* had a walnut-size brain in an elephant-size body.

OTHER ANIMALS
There were other animals just as remarkable as the dinosaurs—flying lobe-finned fish like *Osteolepis*, and a reptilian ancestor of birds, *Archaeopteryx*.

Pteranodon

Archaeopteryx

Osteolepis

Plesiosaurus

Brachiosaurus

Diplodocus

Tyrannosaurus rex

Stegosaurus

Compsognathus

Stenonychosaurus

Corythosaurus

Duckbilled dinosaur

◀ *Like all reptiles, dinosaurs laid eggs. Some skeletons have been found with complete nests. Females may have incubated eggs with their bodies, like some snakes, or buried them as turtles do. The young were born as miniature versions of their parents.*

Deinonychus

HUNTERS AND HUNTED

The largest dinosaurs were plant-eaters. Some species lived in herds for safety. Others, like *Stegosaurus*, relied on armor for defense against predators. The agile, scythe-clawed *Deinonychus* was among the most efficient of dinosaur killers. It may have hunted in groups to kill larger prey.

AFTER THE DINOSAURS

When the dinosaurs vanished, mammals and birds took over the land. *Diatryma* was a large flightless bird, *Smilodon* a saber-toothed big cat. The woolly mammoth was closely related to the modern elephant. All three are extinct.

Woolly mammoth

Diatryma

Smilodon

FACTS ABOUT EXTINCT ANIMALS

• The giant Steppe mammoth that once roamed central Europe, (*Mammuthus trogontherii*), 148 ft. (45 m) tall, was the biggest elephant that has ever lived.
• *Thylacosmilus* looked like the saber-toothed *Smilodon* but was not a cat at all.
• Why dinosaurs vanished is still being debated; climatic changes or an asteroid hitting the Earth are possible causes.
• The earliest ancestor of the horse was the dog-sized *Hyracotherium*, a forest animal of 50 million years ago.
• The Cretaceous pterosaur *Quetzalcoatlus* had wings as long as a bus; these flying reptiles probably had hair, rather than feathers, on the skin that formed their wings.

REPTILE SURVIVORS

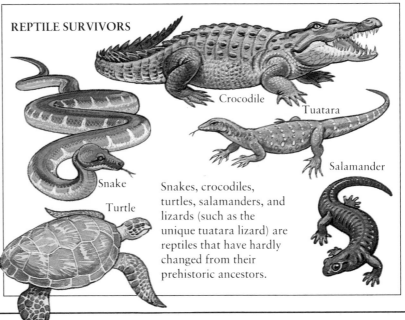

Crocodile

Tuatara

Snake

Salamander

Turtle

Snakes, crocodiles, turtles, salamanders, and lizards (such as the unique tuatara lizard) are reptiles that have hardly changed from their prehistoric ancestors.

THE HUMAN BODY

Systems of the Body

Human beings have more advanced brains than any other living thing. Human brainpower has given us abilities beyond those of any other animal—such as language and the transfer of knowledge from generation to generation. Human beings are primates, members of the species *Homo sapiens sapiens*. We share many characteristics with apes but unlike apes we walk erect on two legs. The body has parts and systems, like a machine, yet it can do things beyond the ability of any machine. It can grow, rebuild, and fight off diseases. The brain is the control center of our bodies; it receives information from our senses and then sends out commands that affect our development, movements, and sensations as well as the involuntary actions of our internal organs. The brain also stores information and is the source of all our feelings, speech, and thoughts.

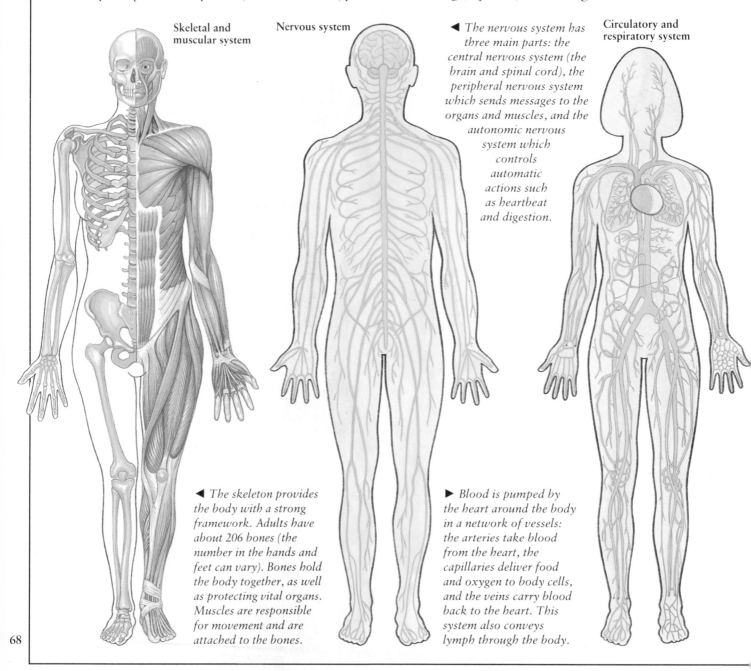

Skeletal and muscular system

Nervous system

Circulatory and respiratory system

◄ *The nervous system has three main parts: the central nervous system (the brain and spinal cord), the peripheral nervous system which sends messages to the organs and muscles, and the autonomic nervous system which controls automatic actions such as heartbeat and digestion.*

◄ *The skeleton provides the body with a strong framework. Adults have about 206 bones (the number in the hands and feet can vary). Bones hold the body together, as well as protecting vital organs. Muscles are responsible for movement and are attached to the bones.*

► *Blood is pumped by the heart around the body in a network of vessels: the arteries take blood from the heart, the capillaries deliver food and oxygen to body cells, and the veins carry blood back to the heart. This system also conveys lymph through the body.*

FACTS ABOUT THE BODY

- The tallest recorded human was Robert Wadlow of the U.S. (1918–1940) who was 8ft. 11.1 in. (2.72 m).
- The oldest human (with an authenticated birth-date) was a Japanese, Shigechiyo Izumi, who died in 1986 aged 120 years 237 days.
- The strongest muscles are the masseters on each side of the mouth, which are used for biting; the most active muscles move the eye.
- An adult's body contains about 10 pints (5 liters) of blood. To pump blood around the body, the heart beats about 70 times a minute.

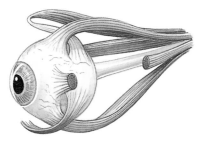

▲ *About 80 percent of the eyeball is made up of a jellylike substance. Six muscles move the eye about in its socket.*

- The fastest nerve signals travel at 250 mph (400 km/h).
- A person takes about 23,000 breaths each day.
- Children have more bones than adults —about 300. As a child grows, some bones fuse together.
- Each of a woman's ovaries contains about 400,000 eggs. Only about 400 mature during her childbearing years.
- The eyeball measures about an inch (25 mm) across.
- There are about 50 million cells in the body and 60,000 miles (100,000 km) of blood vessels.

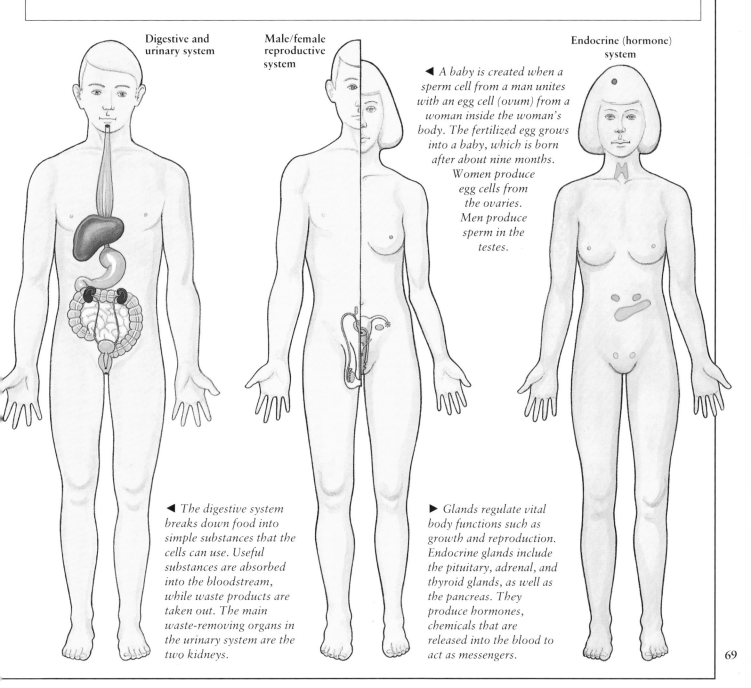

Digestive and urinary system

Male/female reproductive system

Endocrine (hormone) system

◄ *A baby is created when a sperm cell from a man unites with an egg cell (ovum) from a woman inside the woman's body. The fertilized egg grows into a baby, which is born after about nine months. Women produce egg cells from the ovaries. Men produce sperm in the testes.*

◄ *The digestive system breaks down food into simple substances that the cells can use. Useful substances are absorbed into the bloodstream, while waste products are taken out. The main waste-removing organs in the urinary system are the two kidneys.*

► *Glands regulate vital body functions such as growth and reproduction. Endocrine glands include the pituitary, adrenal, and thyroid glands, as well as the pancreas. They produce hormones, chemicals that are released into the blood to act as messengers.*

Skeleton and Muscles

Bones are made of living cells. The largest bone in the body is the femur or thighbone. The smallest is a bone in the ear, the stirrup. The ribs form a cage to protect the heart and lungs; the skull similarly encloses the soft brain. Where bones meet, they form a joint. Joints are held together by elastic ligaments and soft tissue called cartilage. Muscles are attached to the bones by tendons. When the brain orders muscles to contract, the muscles pull the bones—this is how we move.

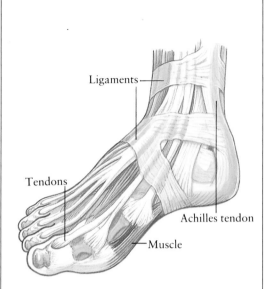

TENDONS AND LIGAMENTS

Tendons and ligaments are tough elastic tissues that hold joints together while allowing them to move. Ligaments connect one bone to another. Tendons connect a muscle to a bone. As the muscle contracts, the tendon acts like a cable, pulling the bone into the new position. In the foot, the Achilles tendon joins the calf muscle to the heel bone. We can consciously control such movements.

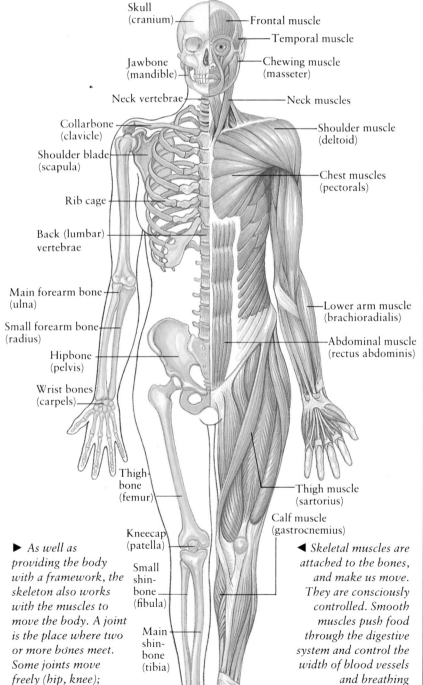

Skull (cranium)
Frontal muscle
Temporal muscle
Jawbone (mandible)
Chewing muscle (masseter)
Neck vertebrae
Neck muscles
Collarbone (clavicle)
Shoulder muscle (deltoid)
Shoulder blade (scapula)
Chest muscles (pectorals)
Rib cage
Back (lumbar) vertebrae
Main forearm bone (ulna)
Small forearm bone (radius)
Lower arm muscle (brachioradialis)
Hipbone (pelvis)
Abdominal muscle (rectus abdominis)
Wrist bones (carpels)
Thigh bone (femur)
Thigh muscle (sartorius)
Kneecap (patella)
Calf muscle (gastrocnemius)
Small shinbone (fibula)
Main shinbone (tibia)

► *As well as providing the body with a framework, the skeleton also works with the muscles to move the body. A joint is the place where two or more bones meet. Some joints move freely (hip, knee); others, such as those in the skull, are fixed.*

◄ *Skeletal muscles are attached to the bones, and make us move. They are consciously controlled. Smooth muscles push food through the digestive system and control the width of blood vessels and breathing passages. They work automatically.*

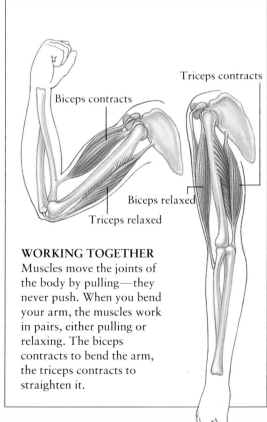

Biceps contracts
Triceps contracts
Biceps relaxed
Triceps relaxed

WORKING TOGETHER

Muscles move the joints of the body by pulling—they never push. When you bend your arm, the muscles work in pairs, either pulling or relaxing. The biceps contracts to bend the arm, the triceps contracts to straighten it.

MUSCLE

The interior of a muscle looks like bundles of cables (*far right*). Skeletal muscle is made up of long cells. Each cell has many nuclei. Smooth muscle and heart (cardiac) muscle both have shorter cells, each with only one nucleus.

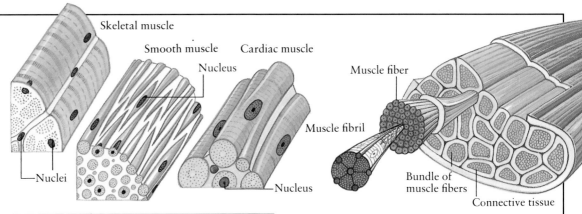

Skeletal muscle

Smooth muscle Cardiac muscle

Nucleus

Nuclei

Nucleus

Muscle fiber

Muscle fibril

Bundle of muscle fibers

Connective tissue

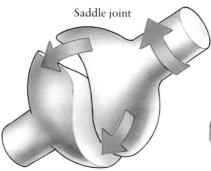
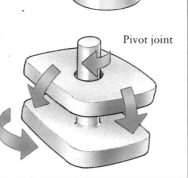

JOINTS

Hinge joints (elbow, knee) allow movement in one direction only. The hip and shoulder are swivelling ball and socket joints. Other joints allow a range of movement: the saddle joint at the base of the thumb, the pivot that allows the forearm to twist, or the plane that allows sideways movement.

Hinge joint

Ball and socket joint

Plane joint

Saddle joint

Pivot joint

INSIDE A BONE

The outer layer of a bone is made up of hard compact bone that forms rings around the Haversian canals. Inside each canal are blood vessels carrying food and oxygen to the bone cells. The compact bone is covered with an even tougher layer, the periosteum. The inner part of a bone is often called the spongy bone, but it is very strong. Bone strength comes from a protein called collagen. The hardness comes from phosphorus and calcium. The soft, fatty core of many bones is called the marrow.

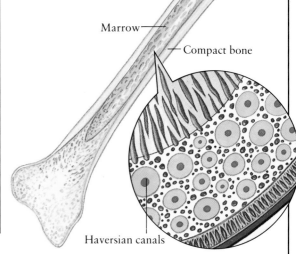

Spongy bone

Periosteum

Marrow

Compact bone

Haversian canals

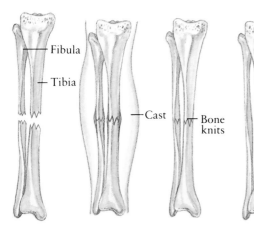

Fibula

Tibia

Cast

Bone knits

◀ *A broken (fractured) bone will heal itself. Doctors set a simple fracture by placing the broken ends together, allowing the repair cells (osteoblasts) to knit the bone together. Compound fractures (with tissue damage) are more serious and the broken bone may need pinning.*

FACTS ABOUT BONES AND MUSCLES

- Bones keep our bodies healthy. The cells of bone marrow produce new blood cells and release them into the bloodstream.
- Muscles make up about 40 percent of a person's body weight.
- When you walk, your body calls over 200 different muscles into use.
- Muscles produce heat when they use energy; this is why people become warm when they exercise.

The Nervous System

The nervous system is a complex network of nerves—bundles of long fibers made up of nerve cells. The nerves collect information from inside and outside the body and send messages to the brain. These messages are signals produced by sensory cells and passed to nerve fibers in the brain or spinal column; signals can also be sent from the brain to the body's organs. The part of the nervous system that controls such automatic body processes as breathing and digestion is called the autonomic nervous system.

▶ *The central nervous system—the brain and spinal cord—carries messages between the brain and body. The peripheral nervous system consists of sensory and motor nerve cells, linked with the central nervous system by special connector cells.*

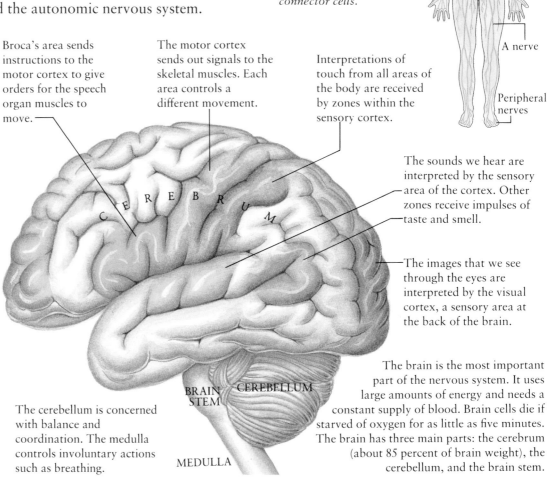

Brain
Spinal cord
A nerve
Peripheral nerves

THE BRAIN
The cortex is in the cerebrum. It receives sense-messages and sends out nerve impulses to the muscles. It is also responsible for conscious feelings, thought, memory, and learning ability. The areas of the brain responsible for conscious thought and speech are at the front of the cortex. The left-hand side of the cortex controls activities on the right of the body; the right side controls the left of the body. The speech, reading, and writing of a right-hander is directed by the left side of the cortex; the right side controls the actions of a left-handed person.

Broca's area sends instructions to the motor cortex to give orders for the speech organ muscles to move.

The motor cortex sends out signals to the skeletal muscles. Each area controls a different movement.

Interpretations of touch from all areas of the body are received by zones within the sensory cortex.

The sounds we hear are interpreted by the sensory area of the cortex. Other zones receive impulses of taste and smell.

The images that we see through the eyes are interpreted by the visual cortex, a sensory area at the back of the brain.

CEREBRUM

BRAIN STEM

CEREBELLUM

MEDULLA

The cerebellum is concerned with balance and coordination. The medulla controls involuntary actions such as breathing.

The brain is the most important part of the nervous system. It uses large amounts of energy and needs a constant supply of blood. Brain cells die if starved of oxygen for as little as five minutes. The brain has three main parts: the cerebrum (about 85 percent of brain weight), the cerebellum, and the brain stem.

EYES AND SIGHT

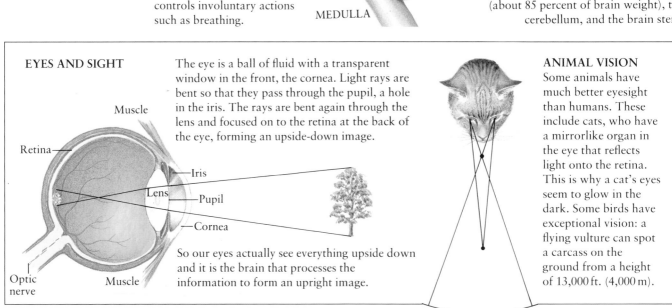

Muscle
Retina
Iris
Lens
Pupil
Cornea
Optic nerve
Muscle

The eye is a ball of fluid with a transparent window in the front, the cornea. Light rays are bent so that they pass through the pupil, a hole in the iris. The rays are bent again through the lens and focused on to the retina at the back of the eye, forming an upside-down image.

So our eyes actually see everything upside down and it is the brain that processes the information to form an upright image.

ANIMAL VISION
Some animals have much better eyesight than humans. These include cats, who have a mirrorlike organ in the eye that reflects light onto the retina. This is why a cat's eyes seem to glow in the dark. Some birds have exceptional vision: a flying vulture can spot a carcass on the ground from a height of 13,000 ft. (4,000 m).

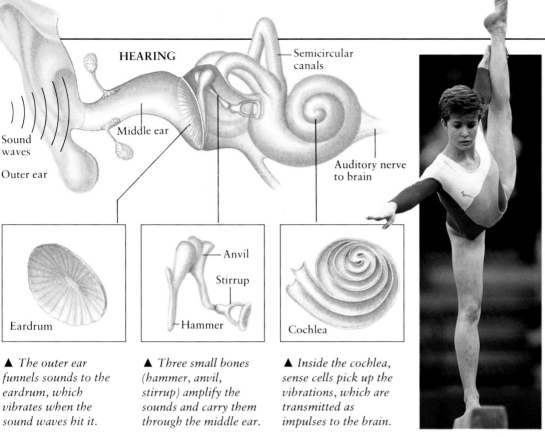

HEARING

Semicircular canals

Sound waves

Outer ear

Middle ear

Auditory nerve to brain

Eardrum

Anvil

Stirrup

Hammer

Cochlea

▲ The outer ear funnels sounds to the eardrum, which vibrates when the sound waves hit it.

▲ Three small bones (hammer, anvil, stirrup) amplify the sounds and carry them through the middle ear.

▲ Inside the cochlea, sense cells pick up the vibrations, which are transmitted as impulses to the brain.

◄ The human ear has three main regions. The inner ear contains three semicircular canals filled with fluid which help us to keep our balance. As you move, the fluid moves. These canals, together with two other sense organs, the utricle and saccule, are called the vestibular organs. They send messages to the brain about the position of the head so that it can direct movements of the muscles that keep the body and the head steady. Any abnormal messages to the brain make a person feel dizzy. Gymnasts (left) must learn to keep their balance.

TOUCH

Touch is a vital sense, because it helps to protect the body from damage. It operates in five ways, sensing pressure, heat, cold, touch, and pain. Receptors are grouped in the dermis layer (see p. 75) of the skin and pass signals to the brain along nerves. The fingertips and lips are among the most sensitive parts of the human body.

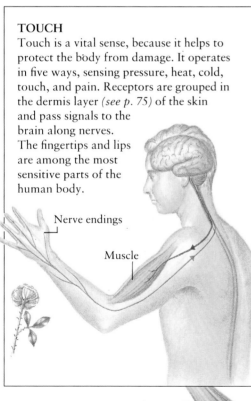

Nerve endings

Muscle

A motor nerve cell

Nucleus

Dendrites

Cell body

Olfactory bulb

Nasal cavity

Sensory nerve to brain

Tongue

Axon

Myelin sheath

Air to lungs and food to stomach

Muscle

▶ A nerve cell, (neurone), has a cell body with fibers branching from it. Short dendrites carry signals to the cell body. A long fiber, or axon, carries messages away from the cell body to the muscle. Messages are passed chemically across the gap between dendrites.

SMELL

Inside the nose are smell receptors. Each has minute hairs covered with sticky mucus. Scent particles dissolve in the mucus, and the receptors send messages to the brain to identify the smell.

TASTE

Taste buds (receptor cells in the tongue) are sensitive to four basic tastes: bitter, sweet, sour, and salt. Different areas of the tongue respond to different tastes. Taste and smell work closely together.

Heart, Blood, and Skin

The heart works continuously to pump blood around the body, through the arteries and veins. The blood carries oxygen from the lungs and food-energy from the food we eat through the arteries to the rest of the body. The veins carry away waste products and return "exhausted" blood from the body to the heart, for the cycle to begin again. The skin acts as a waterproof protective layer, shielding the body from infection and injury; it also keeps the body's internal temperature to a normal level.

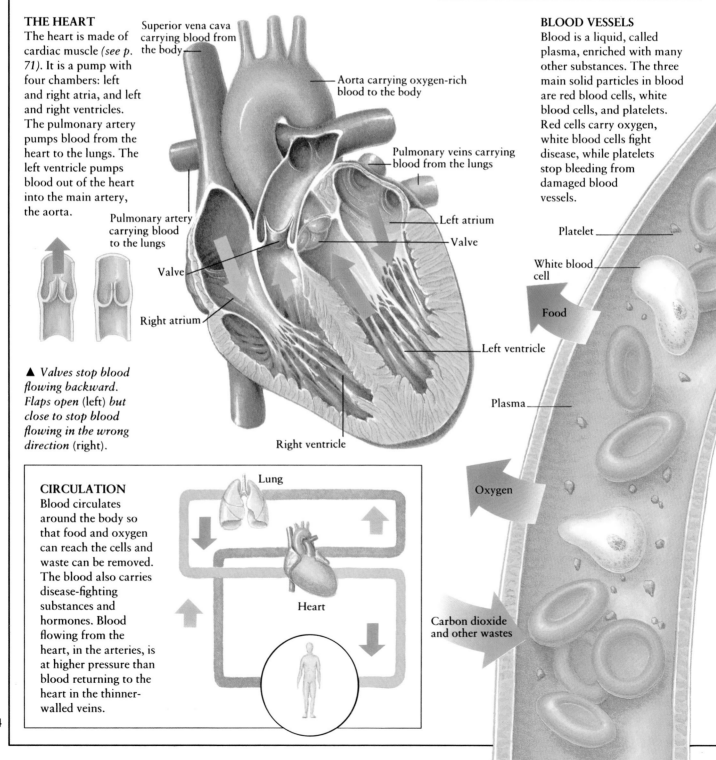

THE HEART
The heart is made of cardiac muscle (see p. 71). It is a pump with four chambers: left and right atria, and left and right ventricles. The pulmonary artery pumps blood from the heart to the lungs. The left ventricle pumps blood out of the heart into the main artery, the aorta.

Superior vena cava carrying blood from the body

Aorta carrying oxygen-rich blood to the body

Pulmonary veins carrying blood from the lungs

Pulmonary artery carrying blood to the lungs

Left atrium

Valve

Valve

Right atrium

Left ventricle

Right ventricle

▲ *Valves stop blood flowing backward. Flaps open (left) but close to stop blood flowing in the wrong direction (right).*

BLOOD VESSELS
Blood is a liquid, called plasma, enriched with many other substances. The three main solid particles in blood are red blood cells, white blood cells, and platelets. Red cells carry oxygen, white blood cells fight disease, while platelets stop bleeding from damaged blood vessels.

Platelet

White blood cell

Food

Left ventricle

Plasma

Oxygen

Carbon dioxide and other wastes

CIRCULATION
Blood circulates around the body so that food and oxygen can reach the cells and waste can be removed. The blood also carries disease-fighting substances and hormones. Blood flowing from the heart, in the arteries, is at higher pressure than blood returning to the heart in the thinner-walled veins.

Lung

Heart

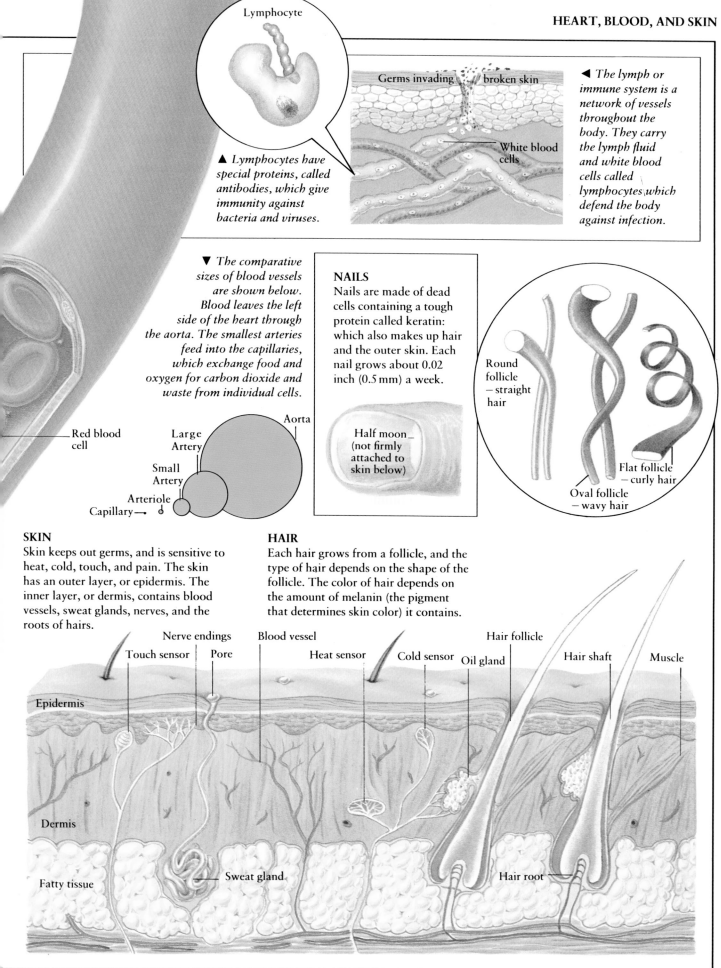

Lymphocyte

▲ Lymphocytes have special proteins, called antibodies, which give immunity against bacteria and viruses.

Germs invading — broken skin

White blood cells

◄ The lymph or immune system is a network of vessels throughout the body. They carry the lymph fluid and white blood cells called lymphocytes which defend the body against infection.

▼ The comparative sizes of blood vessels are shown below. Blood leaves the left side of the heart through the aorta. The smallest arteries feed into the capillaries, which exchange food and oxygen for carbon dioxide and waste from individual cells.

NAILS
Nails are made of dead cells containing a tough protein called keratin: which also makes up hair and the outer skin. Each nail grows about 0.02 inch (0.5 mm) a week.

Red blood cell

Aorta

Large Artery

Small Artery

Arteriole

Capillary →

Half moon (not firmly attached to skin below)

Round follicle – straight hair

Flat follicle – curly hair

Oval follicle – wavy hair

SKIN
Skin keeps out germs, and is sensitive to heat, cold, touch, and pain. The skin has an outer layer, or epidermis. The inner layer, or dermis, contains blood vessels, sweat glands, nerves, and the roots of hairs.

HAIR
Each hair grows from a follicle, and the type of hair depends on the shape of the follicle. The color of hair depends on the amount of melanin (the pigment that determines skin color) it contains.

Nerve endings

Touch sensor   Pore

Blood vessel

Heat sensor   Cold sensor   Oil gland

Hair follicle

Hair shaft   Muscle

Epidermis

Dermis

Fatty tissue

Sweat gland

Hair root

Digestion and Respiration

The digestive system breaks down food into simple substances for the body cells to use. These substances are absorbed into the bloodstream and waste matter is passed out of the body as urine or feces. Cells need oxygen to break down and release the energy in food. The oxygen is taken into the body through the respiratory system—the nose, windpipe, or trachea, and two lungs. You take in oxygen from the air when you breathe in, and release waste carbon dioxide when you breathe out.

BREATHING IN AND OUT
Breathing in: the diaphragm pushes down and the ribs move up and out to increase the chest space. Pressure is then greater outside the lungs than inside, and air moves into them. When breathing out, the process is reversed in order to expel air from the lungs.

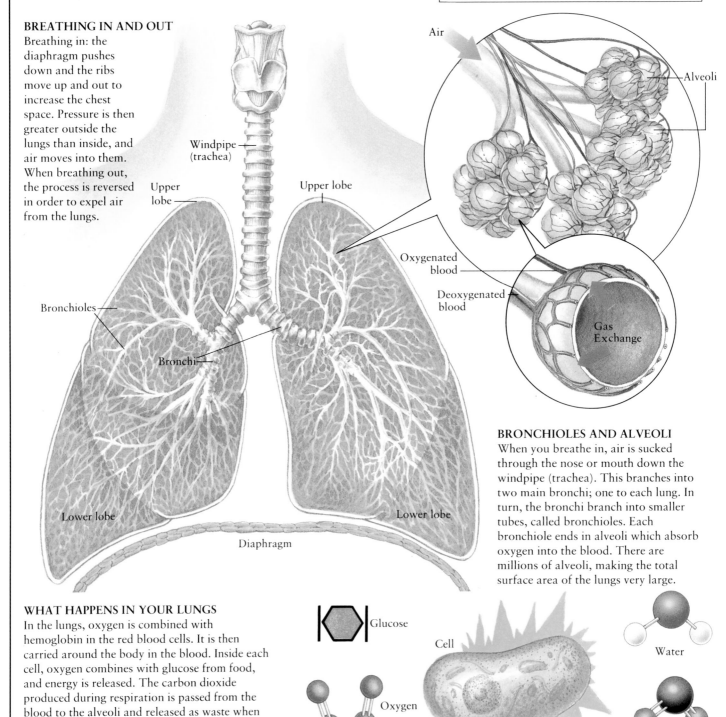

Air

Alveoli

Windpipe (trachea)

Upper lobe

Upper lobe

Bronchioles

Bronchi

Oxygenated blood

Deoxygenated blood

Gas Exchange

Lower lobe

Lower lobe

Diaphragm

BRONCHIOLES AND ALVEOLI
When you breathe in, air is sucked through the nose or mouth down the windpipe (trachea). This branches into two main bronchi; one to each lung. In turn, the bronchi branch into smaller tubes, called bronchioles. Each bronchiole ends in alveoli which absorb oxygen into the blood. There are millions of alveoli, making the total surface area of the lungs very large.

WHAT HAPPENS IN YOUR LUNGS
In the lungs, oxygen is combined with hemoglobin in the red blood cells. It is then carried around the body in the blood. Inside each cell, oxygen combines with glucose from food, and energy is released. The carbon dioxide produced during respiration is passed from the blood to the alveoli and released as waste when we breathe out.

Glucose

Cell

Water

Oxygen

Carbon dioxide

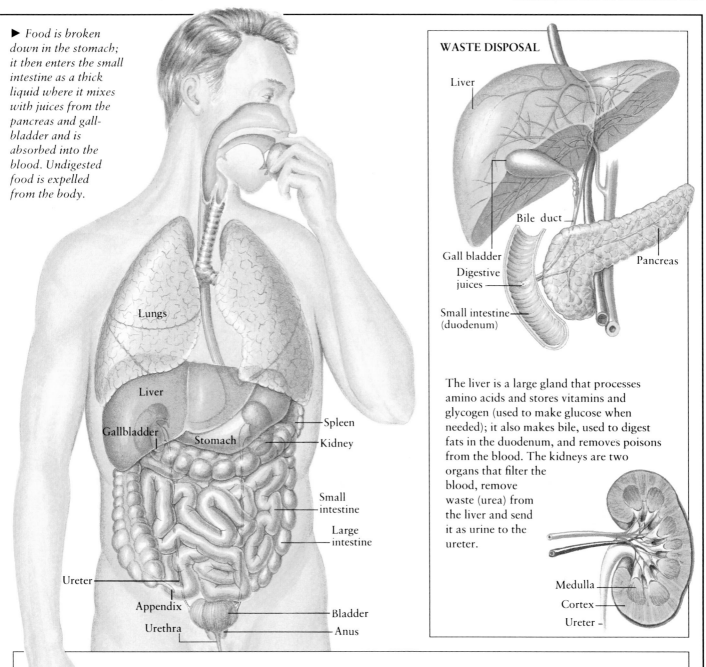

▶ *Food is broken down in the stomach; it then enters the small intestine as a thick liquid where it mixes with juices from the pancreas and gallbladder and is absorbed into the blood. Undigested food is expelled from the body.*

Lungs

Liver

Gallbladder

Stomach

Spleen

Kidney

Small intestine

Large intestine

Ureter

Appendix

Urethra

Bladder

Anus

WASTE DISPOSAL

Liver

Bile duct

Gall bladder

Digestive juices

Small intestine (duodenum)

Pancreas

The liver is a large gland that processes amino acids and stores vitamins and glycogen (used to make glucose when needed); it also makes bile, used to digest fats in the duodenum, and removes poisons from the blood. The kidneys are two organs that filter the blood, remove waste (urea) from the liver and send it as urine to the ureter.

Medulla

Cortex

Ureter

CROSS SECTION OF A MOLAR TOOTH

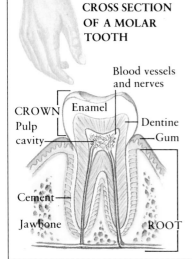

CROWN

Enamel

Pulp cavity

Blood vessels and nerves

Dentine

Gum

Cement

Jawbone

ROOT

TEETH

Teeth prepare food for swallowing and digestion. Some teeth are cutters (incisors), others, grinders (molars). A tooth has three main layers; the outer is made of hard enamel, to resist wear. Underneath lies a hard dentine, over an inner pulpy cavity, which contains nerves and blood vessels. Children have 20 milk (first) teeth; these gradually fall out to be replaced by 32 adult teeth.

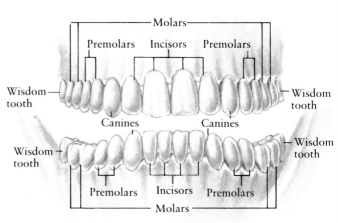

Molars

Premolars   Incisors   Premolars

Wisdom tooth

Wisdom tooth

Canines   Canines

Wisdom tooth

Wisdom tooth

Premolars   Incisors   Premolars

Molars

Reproduction

Humans reproduce sexually, like other mammals. The process of reproduction begins with conception—when sperm from a man fertilizes the egg of a woman. Both egg and sperm contain genetic information in chromosomes, and this information programs the development of the embryo. After about two months the embryo has most of its internal organs. It is now a fetus. At four months, it can move, and after about nine months, a new human being is ready to be born.

The DNA molecule

▲ In the nucleus of each human cell are 32 pairs of chromosomes, made chiefly of proteins and the chemical deoxyribonucleic acid (commonly known as DNA). The DNA molecules contain coded instructions (genes) that control the workings of the cells. These genes also control how the cells develop into a body and carry the code for inherited characteristics.

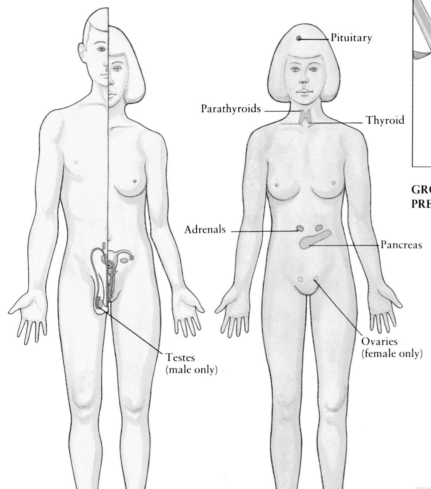

Pituitary

Parathyroids

Thyroid

Adrenals

Pancreas

Testes
(male only)

Ovaries
(female only)

GROWTH DURING PREGNANCY

▼ A human pregnancy typically lasts 38–40 weeks. At 12 weeks the baby is about 4 inches (9 cm) long and weighs 0.5 oz. (14 g).

5 weeks

8 weeks

12 weeks

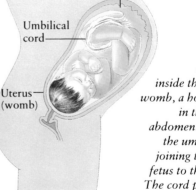

Placenta

Umbilical cord

Uterus (womb)

◀ For 9 months the baby grows inside the uterus, or womb, a hollow organ in the mother's abdomen. Cells form the umbilical cord joining the growing fetus to the placenta. The cord provides the baby with air and food.

FACTS ABOUT REPRODUCTION

• The greatest number of children born in a single birth was 8 girls and 2 boys to a Brazilian woman in 1946.
• The mother who has given birth the most times in recent decades was a woman in Chile who in 1981 produced a final total of 55 children; they included 5 sets of triplets.

▲ The endocrine glands produce hormones. The pituitary hormone regulates growth. Testes produce the male hormone testosterone; ovaries produce the female hormones estrogen and progesterone.

REPRODUCTIVE SYSTEMS

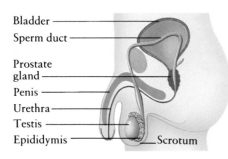

Bladder
Sperm duct
Prostate gland
Penis
Urethra
Testis
Epididymis
Scrotum

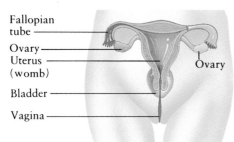

Fallopian tube
Ovary
Uterus (womb)
Bladder
Vagina
Ovary

◀ *The male sex organs (genitals) produce the sexual cell, or sperm. Millions of sperm are made in the male's testes. During sexual intercourse, the sperm move through the urethra and out of the penis and then into the woman's body.*

◀ *An adult woman usually produces one egg a month from her ovaries. The egg passes into the fallopian tubes, and to the uterus. The lining of the uterus thickens, ready to nourish a fertilized egg.*

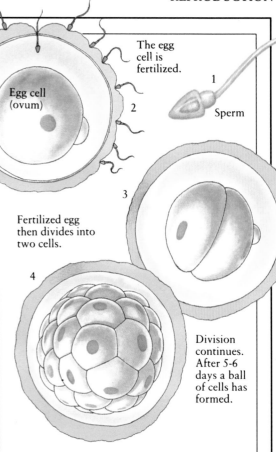

The egg cell is fertilized.

Egg cell (ovum)

1 Sperm

2

3

Fertilized egg then divides into two cells.

4

Division continues. After 5-6 days a ball of cells has formed.

FERTILIZATION

During intercourse, millions of sperm pass from the man's body into the woman's, through the vagina. Only a few hundred reach the fallopian tube, and only one will fertilize the egg. The nuclei of the two cells (male and female) merge, and the cell begins its journey down the fallopian tube to the uterus. On the way, it grows by dividing: one cell becomes 2, 4, 8, 16, and so on.

▼ *By 4 months, the baby has doubled in size. It has well-developed features such as fingers and toes.*

▼ *At 7 months, the baby's lungs and most of its other body organs are working properly. This means that with modern care, the baby will usually survive if it is born prematurely.*

▼ *From 6 to 9 months of a mother's pregnancy, substances in her bloodstream are passed through the placenta that will help the baby to fight off diseases after its birth. At 9 months, the baby is ready to be born.*

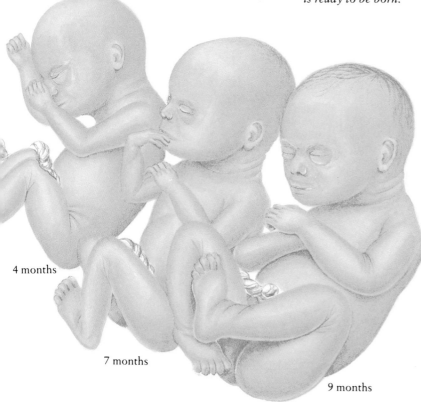

4 months

7 months

9 months

▲ *If the fertilized cell separates into two cells, two babies grow. Identical twins (above) have the same chromosomes, are the same sex and look alike. Two eggs fertilized at the same time by two sperm cells produce non-identical twins, with different chromosomes.*

Growth and Aging

The rate at which children grow never ceases to astonish parents. Humans grow from conception (before birth) until after puberty (about 18–20 years old). Although our bodies do not usually grow taller after that, they do go on changing—putting on or losing weight, for example. Between the ages of 20 and 30 people are at their strongest. As people get older, their body cells renew themselves more slowly, their senses become less acute and they may suffer loss of memory.

AVERAGE NORMAL GROWTH FOR BOYS AND GIRLS

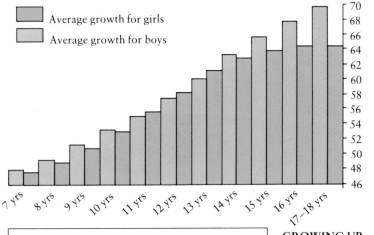

■ Average growth for girls
■ Average growth for boys

Height in inches

7 yrs 8 yrs 9 yrs 10 yrs 11 yrs 12 yrs 13 yrs 14 yrs 15 yrs 16 yrs 17–18 yrs

70
68
66
64
62
60
58
56
54
52
50
48
46

◀ *This chart shows the differences in growth between girls and boys. Girls are on average only heavier and taller than boys around the age of 12 when they start their adolescent growth spurt. By the age of 18 boys are both taller and heavier.*

▲ *Small babies learn to do many things by copying older people; By the time they are 12 months they have begun to stand and say a few words. By 18 months, infants have learned to walk, and play with simple toys such as balls and building blocks.*

Day 1: Uterus lining shed—period begins

Day 5: Uterus lining starts to build up, ready to receive a fertilized egg

Day 14–28: Most likely time for ovum to be fertilized

Day 14: Mature ovum released from ovary

MENSTRUATION
The changes to girls that occur at puberty (usually 9–14) are activated by sex hormones. A girl begins to have periods (a loss of blood). Every month the ovaries of most women of childbearing age release an egg cell. If the egg is not fertilized, it is discharged with some blood and other cells through the vagina; this period of time (3–7 days) is called the menstrual period.

GROWING UP
Humans develop slowly compared to other animals. At birth an average baby is about 20 inches (50 cm) long and weighs nearly 8 pounds (3.5 kg). The infant cannot move and depends on its mother for food, which at first is milk. By the age of two it has tripled in weight. Its hair has grown and it can walk and climb stairs. The baby has teeth and eats solid foods. It can talk and is learning rapidly. In growth, girls outstrip boys briefly around the age of 12, but after that boys grow taller and heavier. Puberty starts later in boys than in girls.

Age two   Age six   Age 10–12

Single cell

Cell grows
larger and prepares
to divide.

SIGNS OF AGING
In boys, one visible sign of developing sexual maturity is the growth of hair on the face (a beard or mustache). This happens any time after the age of 12. Hair also grows around the sexual organs and elsewhere on the body. The voice becomes deeper. With advancing age, other body changes are common. Hair becomes gray, thins, or falls out. The skin wrinkles and muscles begin to sag.

Age 1

Age 30

Cell dividing
into two

CELL RENEWAL
New cells are made by other cells dividing. The two grow to full size and divide again, and so on. This is how all living things grow and repair themselves. In our bodies, more than two million blood cells are made every second to replace old ones dying at the same rate. As we get older, cells renew themselves more slowly, and brain and nerve cells that die are not replaced.

Division complete:
now two identical
cells

Age 70

Age 20–22

Age 30–34

FACTS ABOUT GROWTH

• The average life span in the West and Japan is over 70. Women tend to live longer than men.
• At the age of four a boy is 59 percent adult height, a girl about 64 percent. Boys may carry on growing until they are 23, most girls are fully grown by the age of 20.
• The ovum (female egg cell) is the biggest cell in the body: about the size of a period.
• The heaviest human ever weighed was an American, Jon Minnoch, (1941–1983) who weighed an estimated 1,400 pounds (635 kg) in 1978. He slimmed to 476 pounds (216 kg) by 1979.
• Only one in five people over 100 years old is a man.
• The first "test-tube" baby (conceived outside the mother's body) was Louise Brown, born in Oldham, England, in 1978.

Looking After Your Body

The body can look after itself—it has powerful defenses against disease and amazing powers of repair. But it needs sensible maintenance. Keeping healthy is mostly common sense. Eat a balanced diet of different foods, including fresh fruit and vegetables. Take exercise to keep your body fit and trim (and to enjoy yourself). Avoid harmful habits, such as smoking. Follow basic rules of hygiene (brushing your teeth, washing, taking baths and showers) to keep your whole body clean and healthy.

NUTRITION

Fiber: aids digestion; bread, cereals, vegetables.

Carbohydrates: provide fuel; sugars, starches; bread, cereals, potatoes.

▲ *Nutrition is the process by which the body takes in and uses food. Our diet is the food and drink we eat. A balanced diet should contain some of each of the above foods.*

Fats: provide energy; butter, milk, cheese, eggs, meat, fish, vegetable oils, nuts.

Proteins: provide amino acids; meat, fish, eggs, milk, nuts, bread, potatoes, beans, peas.

WHY WE NEED SLEEP

When you sleep, your heartbeat and breathing slow down, but the brain stays active. Most adults sleep between seven and eight hours a night, although children need more sleep. During sleep, you have periods of dreaming and often change body position.

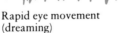

Rapid eye movement (dreaming)

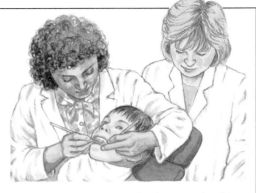

▲ *Regular checkups at the dentist's should ensure your teeth need only minor repairs—such as filling a small cavity.*

FIGHTING TOOTH DECAY

Brushing teeth and gums regularly gets rid of tiny scraps of food sticking to them. This helps to stop tooth decay or cavities, which can cause toothache. Sugars in food and bacteria cause the tooth enamel to decay. Small holes can be filled by the dentist, but badly decayed teeth may have to be taken out.

Cavity

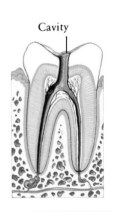

▼ *A fit, healthy body has the stamina to run and play without getting tired quickly.*

Baseball

During sleep the pattern of brain waves records dream periods.

Soccer

HYGIENE AND DISEASE

◀ *Following simple rules of hygiene can help to ward off illness —especially infectious disease. Remember to wash your hands before eating and don't share food and drink. Keep food protected from flies or mice, which leave harmful bacteria.*

DON'T POISON YOUR BODY

Putting poisonous or harmful substances into your body is not a good idea. Smoking cigarettes is known to be a cause of lung cancer. Drinking too much alcohol can seriously damage your body. Taking harmful, habit-forming drugs such as narcotics, barbiturates, tranquilizers, amphetamines, or hallucinogens can damage your health and spoil your enjoyment of life.

▶ *This sign on a bottle or container is a warning that a substance is poisonous and should never be eaten or drunk.*

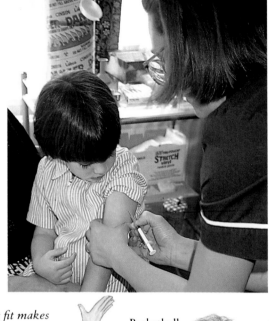

VACCINATION

Vaccination or immunization works by injecting into the body either a harmless form of a poison produced by a disease-bacterium, or a weak form of the bacterium or virus itself. The body's immune system makes antibodies to fight the invading "disease," and these are stored until a real attack by the disease.

▼ *The energy from food builds the strong muscles you need to ride a bike.*

▼ *Keeping fit makes the body supple for energetic movements such as jumping.*

Basketball

KEEPING FIT

You can keep fit in all sorts of enjoyable ways. Take regular exercise, rather than exhausting yourself in one outburst of energy a week. A brisk walk is good for people of all ages. Running, cycling, and swimming are other good ways to keep fit. So is dancing (but not in a smoke-filled room). Some people enjoy gymnastics, or a game of tennis, softball, or football, while others prefer activities such as canoeing, sailing, or climbing.

Tennis

Gymnastics

Bike riding

PLANT GLOSSARY

Algae: Simple, plantlike **organisms**, including single **cells**, giant seaweeds.

Angiosperm: Flowering plant; includes grasses, **herbaceous plants**, most trees.

Annual: Plant that completes its life cycle in a season and then dies.

Anther: Part of the **stamen** (of a flower) that contains **pollen**.

Bark: Tough outer layer of trunk or branch of trees or shrubs.

Berry: Fleshy fruit with no hard inner layer, usually with several seeds; for example, date, orange, raspberry.

Biennial: Plant that completes its life cycle in two seasons, and then dies.

Botany: Scientific study of plants.

Bud: Undeveloped shoot.

Calyx: Protective outer ring of **sepals** of a flower in bud; often greenish, leaflike structures.

Carpel: Flower's female reproductive organ, made up of **stigma**, **style**, and **ovary**.

Cellulose: Tough carbohydrate substance making up the cell walls of plants, formed by chains of **glucose** (sugar) molecules.

Chlorophyll: Green pigment (coloring matter) that enables green plants to use the energy in sunlight to make their food (in **photosynthesis**).

Clone: Plants, such as clusters of bulbs, with identical genetic features produced by **vegetative reproduction**.

Conifers: Cone-producing tree or shrub, usually evergreen.

Corm: Fleshy underground stem in which food is stored.

Cotyledons: Seed leaves forming part of the embryo in a seed.

Cycads: Fernlike tropical plants of the order Cycadales that have existed since prehistoric times; only nine kinds still grow today.

Deciduous: Shedding leaves at the end of each growing season.

Dehiscent fruit: Fruit that bursts open to release seeds; for example, poppies.

Dicotyledon: Member of the class of flowering plants with two **cotyledons** in each seed.

Drupe: Fruit with a fleshy outer layer and a hard inner layer (stone or pit); for example, peach, plum, cherry.

Embryo: Young plant within the seed.

Enzymes: Organic compound produced by plant or animal **cells** that causes chemical reactions in living cells; consists of protein alone or combined with nonprotein organic molecule.

Epidermis: Outer cell layer of a leaf, stem, or root.

Epiphytes: Plants that grow on other plants, but do not feed from them.

Evergreen: Shrub or tree that bears leaves all year round.

Fertilization (in plants): Combining the male reproductive cell with the female ovule to form a seed.

Fruit: Ripe **carpel** or group of carpels, which protects seeds and helps to disperse or spread them.

Fungi: Simple plants without **chlorophyll**; for example, mold, **mushroom**, **yeast**.

Germination: Beginning of growth of a seed or **spore**.

Ginkgos: Plant phylum dating from prehistoric times, now reduced to one species, the **ginkgo** (maidenhair tree).

Glucose: Simple sugar produced in **photosynthesis** and stored as a food reserve by some plants.

Gymnosperm: Term used for plants with seeds unprotected by an **ovary**; collectively **conifers**, **ginkgos**, **cycads**.

Heartwood: Tough wood (with no living **cells**) at the center of a tree that gives the tree its strength.

Herbaceous plant: Plant without a woody stem; part above ground dies down each year, but its roots survive.

Humus: Decaying organic matter in the soil.

Hybrid: *See Animal Glossary*

Legume: Pod or dry fruit produced from a single **ovary**, which splits when ripe; examples include peas, beans, laburnum, clover, acacia.

Lichen: Symbiotic association of **algae** and **fungi**.

Monocotyledon: Flowering plant which has only one **cotyledon** in each seed.

Mushroom: Name used for fruiting bodies of certain **fungi**. Toadstool is another name for mushroom; there is no real difference between them.

Nectar: Liquid made by a flower's nectaries that attracts insects to a flower.

Nut: Fruit containing one seed, within a tough, woody shell.

Order: *see Animal Glossary*

Organic: Having organs or organized physical structure.

Ovary (in flower): Part of the **carpel**, contains the ovules that bear the female reproductive cells.

Parasite: Plant that lives by feeding from another (**host**) plant.

Perennial: Plant that lives for several years.

Petal: Part of flower that attracts pollinators such as birds or insects.

Phloem: Tissue that conducts food and other materials through a plant.

Photosynthesis: Process by which plants use sunlight to convert water and carbon dioxide into food (sugar).

Pistil: Another word for the female part of a flower (the **carpel**).

Pollen: Mass of grains made in the **stamens** of a flower, carrying male reproductive cells.

Pollination: Transfer of **pollen** from **stamen** to **stigma**.

Respiration: Taking in oxygen from the air to "burn" food to provide energy, releasing carbon dioxide.

Rhizoid: Hairlike structure anchoring a moss to the ground.

Runner: Creeping stem by which plants such as strawberries reproduce.

Saprophyte: Organism that feeds on chemicals from decaying plants or animals; many **fungi** are saprophytes.

Sepal: Outermost parts of a flower, usually green; they protect **petals** before flower opens.

Shrub: Woody plant with many branches.

Species: *see Animal Glossary.*

Spore: Single or multi-celled structure formed during reproductive process in many plants; for example, ferns, **mushrooms**.

Stamen: Male reproductive part of a flower, made up of **anther** and supporting stalk or filament.

Starch: Carbohydrate made up of sugars, the main food storage compound in plants; potato tubers store starch.

Stigma: Tip of the **carpel** of a flower, receives the **pollen**.

Style: Stalklike part of the **carpel**, with **stigma** at its tip.

Succulents: Plants with swollen leaves, for storing water.

Symbiosis: *see Animal Glossary.*

Taproot: Main root of a plant.

Tendril: Modified stem, leaf or leaflet used by some climbing plants to coil around any support.

Thallus: Simple plant body not divided into root, stem, and leaves.

Transpiration: Loss of water by evaporation from a plant's leaves.

Tuber: Swollen stem used to store food.

Vegetative reproduction: Process in which a whole new plant is produced from part of a plant with sexual reproduction; for example, a bulb.

Xylem: Woody tissue.

Yeasts: Single-celled **fungi**, many of which can cause fermentation (used in baking, brewing, and wine-making).

ANIMAL GLOSSARY

Albino: Animal lacking pigment from its skin, hair, feathers, or eyes.

Amphibian: Animal that lives partly in water and partly on land.

Anatomy: Study of the internal structure of living organisms.

Antenna: Sense-organ on the head of an **arthropod**.

Arthropod: Animal with hard external skeleton, segmented body, and jointed limbs; includes insects, **arachnids**, **crustaceans**, centipedes, millipedes.

Aquatic: Living in water.

Arachnid: Arthropod, normally with four pairs of walking legs, no antennae and a pair of grasping appendages on the head; for example spiders, scorpions.

Bacterium (plural bacteria): Microscopic single-celled organism. Most are harmless, but some cause disease. **Bacteria** help to break down dead plant and animal remains.

Barbel: Slender sensory **organ** that grows from the jaws of some fishes.

Benthic: Living on the seabed.

Biome: Major community of plants and animals, characterized by a particular type of vegetation (for example, savanna, rain forest) and climate.

Biological control: Control of pests by use of natural predators or diseases; for example, use of **bacteria** to control grain weevils and use of fish to control mosquitoes.

Biosphere: Part of the Earth and atmosphere that is inhabited by living **organisms**.

Blubber: Thick layer of fat under the skin of a whale or seal.

Camouflage: Disguise, produced by color, pattern, or shape, that makes an animal hard to see.

Carnivore: Animal that lives by eating meat rather than plants.

Carrion: Remains or flesh of an animal that has died.

Cartilage: Tough, elastic gristle in animal bodies; a layer of cartilage makes joints work smoothly. In sharks and rays, the skeleton is made of cartilage rather than bone.

Caterpillar: Soft-bodied **larva** that is a stage in the development of certain kinds of insect; for example, moths and butterflies.

Cell: Structural and functional unit that makes up all living things. There are many types of cell; for example, bone cells, skin cells, nerve cells.

Class: Grouping of living things, the next major rank below **phylum**.

Classification: Way in which animals and plants are divided into groups and subgroups.

Clutch: Set of eggs laid by a bird.

Cold-blooded: Animal that cannot automatically keep its body at operating temperature by burning fuel (sugar) stored in the body. A cold-blooded animal remains at about the same temperature as its surroundings.

Colony: Large number of animals living together; ants, rabbits, seals, and gulls all live in colonies.

Convergence: Resemblance between animals of different species that has developed because they adapted to the same kind of life in different parts of the world; examples are the Australian spiny anteater and the European hedgehog.

Coral: Small sea animals called polyps that grow in a hard, chalky skeleton. They often live in a **colony** and their remains form coral reefs.

Courtship: Behavior that leads up to two animals pairing and mating.

Crustacean: **Arthropods** such as crabs and shrimps; they almost all live in water and most have a shell.

Dinosaur: Prehistoric reptile known only from **fossils**. Dinosaurs of many kinds were the major land animals between 205 and 65 million years ago.

Display: Any kind of animal behavior that has a particular meaning. For example, **courtship** display is used to attract a mate; threat display is used to frighten off an enemy.

Diurnal: Animal active by day, rather than by night. *See also* **nocturnal**

Dorsal: Of or close to the back of an animal; for example, the dorsal fin of a fish.

Echinoderm: Marine **invertebrates**, symmetrical in shape, often with spiny skins; they have "tube feet" for movement or feeding. They include starfish and sea urchins.

Ecology: Study of the relationship between plants and animals.

Ecosystem: Community of **organisms** and the **habitat** in which they live.

Embryo: Immature **organism** developing in the egg or in the womb of its mother.

Evolution: Changes that take place in animal and plant **species**, over millions of years, that change them from simpler to more complex forms.

Exoskeleton: External **skeleton** or outer body that covers the body of animals such as **arthropods**.

Extinct (of animals or plants): **Family** or **species** that has died out.

Family: Grouping used in the **classification** of animals and plants. Similar families are grouped together in an **order**.

Fauna: Animal population of a particular area or period in time.

Feral: Animals (such as cats) that have escaped from homes or captivity and are living wild.

Food chain: Natural links between animals and what they eat. A simple example is cat-bird-spider-fly—each one eats the next one down the chain.

Fossil: Remains of an animal or plant left in rocks. The best fossils are found in limestone and mudstone.

Genus (plural genera): Grouping used in the **classification** of living **organisms**. Similar genera are grouped together in a **family**. A genus is divided into **species**.

Gill: Breathing organ of animal, such as a fish, that lives in water; it takes oxygen from the water just as animals with lungs take oxygen from air.

Habitat: Natural living place of an animal or plant. Examples are lakes, forests, grassland, deserts.

Herbivore: Plant-eating animal.

Hibernate: To spend the winter in a deep sleep; the animal slows down its heartbeat and other body systems and lives off stored body fat until spring.

Host: Animal or plant that is used by another animal or plant as a source of food. The **parasite** lives on, or in some cases inside, the host.

Hybrid: Plant or animal produced from the mating of parents of different species or varieties; hybrids between species are usually sterile. A mule, for example, is the offspring of a horse and a donkey that have mated.

Insectivore: Insect-eating animal; many insectivores eat other **invertebrates** as well as insects.

Instinct: Built-in ability to do certain things without having to learn them; for example, baby turtles always go to the sea as soon as they hatch out.

Invertebrate: Animal that does not have a backbone; for example, **arthropods**.

Kingdom: Largest grouping used in the classification of living **organisms**.

Larva: Grub of an insect; the insect is a larva from when it hatches from the egg until it turns into a **pupa**.

Life cycle: Series of stages through which an **organism** passes from **fertilization** to death.

Mammal: Warm-blooded **vertebrate** with a larger brain and greater intelligence than other types of animal; all mammals suckle their young and have a covering of hair.

Marsupial: Mammal whose young are born in an undeveloped state. The young complete their development inside their mother's pouch.

Mating season: Time of year when male and female animals pair off, or gather in groups, in order to breed.

Metamorphosis: Means "change of shape" and describes the changes in an insect's life from egg to **larva** to **pupa** to adult. At each change, the insect grows a new kind of body.

Migrate: To make a regular journey to a particular place in order to breed and raise young, or in some cases to search out better food supplies.

Mollusk: Large group of **invertebrate** animals that usually have hard shells; includes snails, slugs, squids, and octopuses.

Monotreme: Egg-laying mammal with other reptilian features; includes platypus and echidna.

Natural selection: Natural process in which the animals best equipped for a particular set of living conditions will be the most successful breeders.

Nocturnal: Animals active at night. *See also* **diurnal**

Nucleus: Central part of an animal or plant **cell** that acts as a command center and controls all the chemical processes the cell carries out.

Nymph: Immature insect, resembling the adult but without wings.

Omnivore: Animal that has wide diet, including meat and plants.

Order: Grouping used in the **classification** of plants and animals. Similar orders are grouped together in a **class**. Order is divided into **families**.

Organism: Any living thing, plant or animal.

Parasite: Plant or animal that depends completely on another plant or animal in order to stay alive.

Pelagic: Living in the upper regions of the ocean.

Phylum: In animal and plant **classification**, a group below **kingdom**.

Placental mammals: Mammals whose young are well developed inside the mother before they are born. The placenta is the organ that supplies the unborn baby with food.

Plankton: Tiny animals that drift in salt or fresh water.

Predator: **Carnivore** that gets food by hunting and killing other animals.

Prehistoric: Something that dates from before history, or before the invention of writing.

Primary feathers: Flight feathers on the parts of a bird's wing that correspond to the human wrist, palm, and fingers.

Primate: Mammal of the group that includes monkeys, apes, and humans; called the primate or "first" because it is the highest **order** of mammals.

Protein: Any of a group of complex compounds of hydrogen, oxygen, and nitrogen, and sometimes other elements. Proteins are essential parts of all living **cells**.

Protozoan: Simple single-celled **organisms** considered to be animal-like; currently classified in the kingdom Protoctista.

Pupa: Stage between the **larva** and adult in the development of some insects.

Raptor: Predatory bird adapted for seizing prey; for example, hawk, owl.

Regeneration: When a living thing regrows or replaces lost **organs** or tissues.

Reproduction: Process of making new members of the same animal or plant species. Some species reproduce asexually by growing an additional replica of the parent, or by splitting into two identical copies. Others reproduce sexually by joining together an egg from a female parent and sperm from the male parent.

Reptile: Cold-blooded scaly animals that lay eggs on land; a few give birth to live young. Reptiles include snakes, lizards, crocodiles, turtles, tortoises.

Rodent: Mammals with big, chisel-like, front teeth used for gnawing tough plant food. Rodents include mice, squirrels, beavers, porcupines.

Ruminant: Animal such as cow, goat, or sheep that has a four-chambered stomach that enables it to process tough plant food. Ruminants feed, then later bring up the food into their mouths and chew it a second time.

Scavenger: Animal that feeds on refuse or the flesh of dead animals (**carrion**); for example, jackals, vultures, beetles.

Skeleton: Framework of bone that supports the body of a bird, **mammal**, fish, **amphibian**, or **reptile**. *See also* **Exoskeleton**

Spawn: Eggs without hard shells that are laid in large quantities by fish, **amphibians**, or **mollusks**.

Species: Group of animals or plants of the same kind that breed and produce more of their own kind. Species of the thrush family, for example, are quite different from species of the heron family.

Symbiosis: Association between two dissimilar living organisms from which both partners benefit.

Terrestrial: Living on land.

Territory: Area of land that animal (usually the male) takes over and defends against other animals of the same species.

Thorax: Middle section of an insect's body, between the head and the abdomen. The thorax carries three pairs of legs and two pairs of wings.

Tundra: Arctic region of level, treeless, land; has thin soil that is always frozen, apart from the surface layer, which melts in summer so that a carpet of grass and lichen can grow.

Ungulate: **Herbivores** with hooves such as horses and cows.

Vertebrate: Animal with a backbone; vertebrates have an internal **skeleton** of bone and **cartilage**, or just cartilage, a spinal cord, a brain enclosed in a cranium, a **heart** with 2–4 chambers, and a maximum of 4 limbs. *See also* **Invertebrate**

Warm-blooded: Animal that maintains its body at full operating temperature by burning fuel (food) to create chemical energy; warm-blooded animals keep themselves warm in cold weather (within certain limits) and cool in hot weather.

Wattles: Fleshy parts on the chin or throat of a bird such as a turkey.

Zoo: Public or private grounds where animals are kept for study and/or exhibition to the public.

Zoogeography: Study of the geographical distribution of animals.

Zoology: Study of animals.

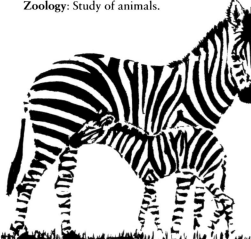

HUMAN BODY GLOSSARY

Abscess: Painful, red, swollen area, inside the body, caused by **bacteria**.

Acne: Pimples, blackheads, or whiteheads caused by inflammation of the oil glands in the skin.

Acupuncture: Chinese medical treatment, relying on the pricking of skin with needles in the parts of the body where the Chinese believe the life forces flow.

Adenoids: Small **glands** at the back of the nasal passages.

Allergy: Reaction such as a running nose, rash, or wheezing caused when people are sensitive to certain substances such as dust or pollen.

Anesthetic: Substance that makes a person insensitive to pain. A general anesthetic puts a person to sleep before an operation. A local anesthetic numbs only the area of the body where the drug was applied.

Antibiotics: Drugs that can kill **bacteria**. Antibiotics do not kill **viruses** and so cannot cure viral diseases such as the common cold.

Antibodies: Substances produced by the body's immune system. They destroy harmful **bacteria** and **viruses**.

Antiseptics: Substances used to clean wounds and sterilize doctors' instruments; they prevent the growth of disease carrying microorganisms.

Artery: Any blood vessel which carries blood away from the heart to the rest of the body.

Asthma: Difficulty in breathing, usually caused by an **allergy** or infection.

Autonomic nervous system: Part of the nervous system that controls "automatic" actions such as breathing and heartbeat.

Backbone: Another word for the spine or vertebral column.

Bile: Green liquid produced by the **liver** that helps to digest fat. Bile is stored in the **gall bladder**.

Bladder: Muscular bag that collects urine produced by the **kidneys**.

Blood pressure: Measured using a sphygmomanometer. The results are shown as two figures given in millimeters of mercury—a person's blood pressure should range from 100–140 mm when their heart contracts, 60–90 mm when it relaxes.

Brain: Organ of mass of nerve **tissue**; in humans, the center of the nervous system, occupying the entire skull.

Bruise: Mark on the skin caused by a bang or by pressure; blood vessels under the skin are damaged.

Cancer: Disease that begins when some abnormal or malignant **cells** begin to grow uncontrolledly and form a tumor or swelling.

Capillary: Blood vessel connecting the small branches of **arteries** with small branches of **veins**.

Carbohydrates: With **protein** and fats, one of the three main groups of foods. Foods which contain a lot of carbohydrate are bread, cereals, potatoes, and rice.

Cartilage: *See* **Animal Glossary**

Cholesterol: A fatty substance made by the **liver** and adrenal **glands**.

Chromosome: One of the 46 structures in the nucleus of every **cell**. Chromosomes are made of **DNA**; they carry the genes that determine inherited characteristics.

Coronary: Referring to the blood vessels that supply the **heart**.

Corpuscle: Another name for a red or white blood cell.

Cortex: Outer layer of the **brain** or "gray matter," responsible for all thinking processes.

Cramp: Pain in a **muscle**, caused when it contracts and goes into a spasm.

Dermis: Lower living layer of the skin—just below the epidermis.

Diabetes: Illness in which a person does not produce enough **insulin** and so cannot control the level of sugar (**glucose**) in their blood.

DNA: Deoxyribonucleic acid is the chemical that makes up our chromosomes and carries—as **genes**—all the information which we inherit from our parents.

Eardrum (tympanum): Thin membrane at the end of the ear canal.

Eczema: Inflammation of the skin (itchy rash and blisters).

Esophagus: Tube that carries food from the mouth to the stomach.

Eustachian tube: Tube that connects the middle ear with the throat; it helps to keep the pressure inside the ear the same on both sides of the **eardrum**.

Feces: Waste material that leaves the body after food has been digested.

Femur: Thigh bone—the longest, strongest bone in the body.

Fertilization (in animals): Union of two unlike sexual **cells** or **gametes** (**sperm** and **ovum**). In humans, this may happen between the 13th and 15th day of a woman's **menstrual cycle**, in one of the Fallopian tubes; after it has been fertilized the ovum can begin to develop into a baby.

Fetus: Unborn baby from two months until it is born. From **fertilization** to two months it is called an embryo.

Fingerprints: No two people have the same fingerprints, which is why police use them as a means of identification.

Follicle: Pocket in the skin from which hair grows.

Gall bladder: Sac, about 3–4 inches (8–10 cm) long, under the **liver**, that releases **bile**.

Gamete: Mature **cell** that can unite with another in sexual reproduction.

Genes: Combinations of fundamental **DNA** units that make up the **chromosomes** in each **cell**.

Glands: The body has two types of glands: exocrine produce substances that are carried away in ducts, endocrine produce **hormones** that are secreted into the blood.

Heart: Muscular organ that keeps blood circulating through the body.

Hemoglobin: Red pigment found in **red blood cells** that gives blood its color. Hemoglobin carries oxygen from the **lungs** around the body to the **cells**.

Hormones: The body's chemical messengers—substances produced in tiny amounts in the endocrine **glands**; they control many body processes.

Hypothermia: Especially low body temperature that occurs when a person is too cold for too long.

Immunization: Way of preventing certain diseases, usually by giving injections.

Insulin: Hormone produced by the **pancreas** that controls the level of **glucose** (sugar) in the blood.

Intestine: Long tube, beginning at the stomach and ending at the anus, in which food is digested.

Iris: Colored part of the eye that surrounds the pupil.

Joint: Place where two bones meet; lined with **cartilage** and held in place by **ligaments**.

Keratin: Hard substance found in nails, hair, and skin.

Kidneys: Organs that filter waste from the blood and produce urine, which collects in the **bladder**.

Larynx (voice box): Located at the top of the **trachea**, it is made of **cartilage** and has the vocal cords inside it.

Ligament: Tough elastic band of **tissue** that holds bones together at a **joint**.

Liver: The body's largest **gland** is found in the abdomen of **vertebrates**; an adult's liver weighs about 3 pounds

(1,500 g). The liver's functions include the secreting of **bile**.

Lymph: Clear liquid that contains **white blood cells**.

Lungs: **Organs** that enable air-breathing vertebrates to breathe.

Marrow: Soft, jellylike substance in the hollow centers of some bones.

Membranes: Thin layers of **cells** that line or cover various parts of the body. Membranes line the nose, mouth, and **intestine**, and cover the **heart**, **lungs**, and other **organs**. Many lining membranes produce mucus to protect the body—in particular its openings—from infection.

Menstruation (or periods): Bleeding from the **vagina** as the lining of the **uterus** breaks down during the female menstrual cycle. *See also* **Fertilization**

Muscle: Tissue that effects movement of the body. There are three types of muscles in the body: skeletal or striped muscle allows for movement; heart muscle pumps blood around the body; smooth muscle in the intestine moves food.

Nerves: Bundles of the long fibers of nerve cells that carry electrical messages to and from the brain and **spinal cord**.

Organ: Group of different tissues that work together to perform a special job in the body. For example, the **kidneys, heart** and **lungs**.

Ovaries: Two female **organs** that produce ova (egg cells). Usually one is released each month from puberty to menopause (about 11 years to between 45–55 years).

Pancreas: **Gland** behind the stomach; it produces **insulin**, and pancreatic juice, which helps to digest food in the duodenum (small intestine).

Pelvis: Hip bones.

Pituitary gland: Endocrine **gland** at the base of the brain.

Plasma: Liquid part of blood that remains when **red** and **white blood cells** and platelets are removed.

Plastic surgery: Surgery, usually for repairing or rebuilding parts of the body that have been damaged or scarred.

Proteins: Body-building chemicals that are part of every living **cell**. Proteins are made of units called amino acids.

Puberty: When reproductive system becomes active; begins between 12–15 years for a boy and between 10–14 years for a girl.

Pulse: Throbbing that can be felt in arteries as the heart pumps. For adults pulse rate is 65–80 beats per minute, for a 10-year-old about 90 beats per minute, and for a baby about 140 beats per minute.

Red blood cells: Small disk-shaped cells in the blood that carry oxygen to all cells.

Renal: Referring to the **kidneys**.

Retina: Inner lining of the eyeball that is sensitive to light.

Saliva: Liquid produced by three pairs of **glands** in the mouth. Saliva moistens food so that it can be swallowed easily and it contains an enzyme (ptyalin) that digests starch.

Siamese twins: Identical twins who are joined together when they are born.

Sinuses: Hollow cavities inside the skull; there are two sets in the forehead, one behind the nasal passages and one in the cheeks.

Sneeze: Reflex action that forces air out of the **lungs** through the nose in order to clear an irritation in the nasal passages.

Sperm: Male sex cells that are produced in the **testes**.

Spinal cord: Thick cord of nerves that extends from the base of the **brain** to the bottom of the back.

Spleen: Soft **organ** on the left side of the body between the stomach and diaphragm. In adults it is part of the **lymph** system and helps fight infection.

Tendons: Bands of **tissue** that connect **muscles** to bones.

Testes: Two male sex glands that produce **sperm** cells and male **hormones**.

Thyroid: **Gland** in the neck, on both sides of the **trachea**, that produces the growth **hormone** thyroxine.

Tissues: Groups of similar **cells** that form various parts of the body.

Tonsils: Oval structures found at the entrance to the throat. Together with the **adenoids** they guard against the **bacteria** that may enter through the mouth and nose.

Trachea (windpipe): Leads from the **larynx** in the throat to the two main bronchi in the chest.

Tumor: Swelling caused by the abnormal growth of cells without a useful function. There are two kinds of tumor: malignant (invading normal tissue; cancerous) or benign (non-malignant).

Ulcer: Open sore on the skin or on a membrane inside the body.

Umbilical cord: Cord that connects a developing baby to the placenta inside its mother's **uterus**.

Ureters: Tubes that carry urine from the **kidneys** to the **bladder**.

Urethra: Tube that leads from the **bladder** to the outside of the body.

Uterus (womb): Part of a woman's body, inside her abdomen, where a baby develops.

Vaccination: Injecting a person with weakened or dead disease-causing microorganisms to make them immune from one or several diseases.

Vagina: Passageway from the **uterus** to the outside of a female mammal's body. During childbirth it stretches to let the baby out.

Vein: Any blood vessel that carries blood toward the **heart**.

Villi: Tiny projections from the lining of the small intestine that absorb digested food.

Virus: Infectious agent capable of causing illness in plants and animals; infectious diseases include measles, mumps, poliomyelitis, and smallpox.

Vitamins: Group of substances found in food that are essential for health. An average person needs small amounts of about 15 different vitamins.

Vocal cords: Two ligaments stretched across the **larynx**, controlled by **muscles** that allow speech.

White blood cells: Colorless **cells** in blood that help to fight disease; they are larger than **red blood cells** and are made in the bone **marrow**.

Zygote: **Cell** that results from the fusion of two **gametes**; a fertilized egg before it begins to divide

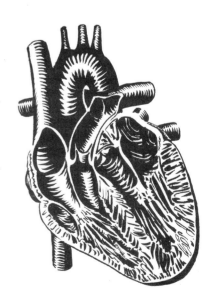

INDEX

Page numbers in *italic* type refer to illustrations or map references

Page numbers in **bold** type refer to key topics

A

Aardvarks 53, *53*
Adder's-tongue *21*
Aging (human) 80–81, *80–81*
Albatrosses 50, *50*, 51
Algae 10, *11*, 13, 16, 18, *18*, 19, *19*, 84
Alligator gar 42, *42*
Alligators 46, 47, *47*, 63

Alpine habitat 15, *15*, 25, *25*
Alpine swift *49*
Amphibians *10*, 44–45, *44–45*, 85
Anacondas 47, *47*
Anglerfish 43, *43*
Animal kingdom, The 34–67, *34–67*;
   amphibians 44–45, *44–45*
   animal homes 56–57, *56–57*
   animal movement 58–59, *58–59*
   animals and people 62–63, *62–63*
   animals and their young 60–61, *60–61*
   arthropods 38–39, *38–39*; *see also*
   insects
   bird behavior 50–51, *50–51*
   birds 48–49, *48–49*
   endangered animals 64–65, *64–65*
   fish 42–43, *42–43*
   insects 40–41, *40–41*
   invertebrates, marine 36–37, *36–37*
   mammal senses 54–55, *54–55*
   mammals 52–53, *52–53*
   phyla 34–35, *34–35*

prehistoric animals 66–67, *66–67*
   reptiles 46–47, *46–47*
Annelids 34, *34*
Anteaters 55, *55*
Anthers 26, *26*
Ants 41, *41*, 61
Apples 32, *32*
Arachnids 35, 38, *38*, 39, *39*, 56, 58, 61, 63
Archaeopteryx 66, *66*
Arctic habitat 14, 15
Armadillos 53, *53*
Arthropods 35, *35*, 38–39, *38–39*, 85
Asses 62, *62*
Axolotls 45, *45*

B

Bacteria 10, *11*, 13, 16, 18, 32, 85
Bamboos 17, *17*
Banyan trees 31, *31*
Baobabs 31, *31*
Barn owl *49*
Bats 35, *35*, 53, *53*, 55, *55*, 56, *56*
Beans 24, 28, *28*
Bearded saki 64, *64*
Bears 60, *60*
Beavers 56, *56*
Bee-eaters 56, *56*
Bees 27, 40, *40*, 62, *62*
Beetles 41, *41*
Berries 29, *29*
Bills (birds) 50, *50*
Biomes *see* habitats
Bird-eating spider 39, *39*
Birds *10*, 48–51, *48–51*, 59, 60, 63, 64, 65, 67
Bison, European 64, *64*
Bivalves 37, *37*
Blackberries 29, *29*
Black swan *48*
Black widow spider 39, *39*
Bladderwrack 18, *18*
Blood (human) 68, *68*, 69, 74, *74*, 87
Bluebell 24, *24*
Blue whale 35, *35*
Bones (human) 68, *68*, 70, *70*, 71, *71*
Bonsai 31, *31*
Bootlace worms 36
Brachiopods *10*
Brain (human) 72, *72–73*, 87
Breathing *see* respiration
Bristlecone pines 31, *31*
Bulb plants 24, 26, *26*, 28, 33
Bumblebee bats 35, *35*
Butterflies 40–41, *40–41*, 59, 64–65
Butterfly fish 43, *43*

C

Cacti 17, *17*, 25, *25*
Caecilians 44, 45, *45*
Caimans 47, *47*
Camels 62, *62*
Carmine bee-eaters 56, *56*
Carnivores 55, *55–56*, 85
Carnivorous plants 27, *27*
Carrots 24, 28, *28*
Caterpillars 40, *40*, 85
Catfish 43, *43*
Cats 54, 61, 63, 64, *64*, 67, *67*
Cattle 62, *62*
Cauliflowers 28, *28*
Cedar of Lebanon *23*
Cell division 81, *81*
Centipedes 35, *35*, 38, *38*
Cereals 24, 28
Chameleons 46, *46*
Chestnuts 29
Chimpanzees 55, *55*
Cinchona tree 32, *32*
Chlorophyll 26, 30, 32, 84
Chordates 35, *35*
Chrysalis 40, *40*
Chub 43, *43*
Cichlids 43, *43*
Clams 36, *36*, 37, 61
Classes (classification) 12, 13, 85;
   of mammals 53
Classification 12–13, *12–13*, 16, 85
Cleaner wrasse 43, *43*
Club mosses 17, *17*, 20, 21
Coast redwood *23*
Cobras 46, *46*
Cockroaches 40
Cockscomb *18*
Coelacanths 42, *42*
Coelenterates *11*
Colonies, animal 56, 85
Colugo 53
Composite flowers 26, *26*
Conifers *11*, 17, 22–23, 25, 31, 84
Coral 36, *36*, 43, 85
Coral polyps 34, *34*
Coral snake 46
Cork 32, *32*
Corms 26, *26*
Corn 28, 29
Corn bunting 50, *50*
Cotton 32, *32*
Courtship 45, 51, 60, 85
Cows 55, 62, *62*
Crabs 35, *35*, 38, *38*, 39
Crane, black crowned *48*
Crocodiles 46, 47, *47*, 63, *63*, 67, *67*
Crossbills 50, *50*
Cross-breeding of plants 32

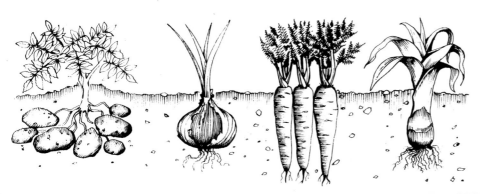

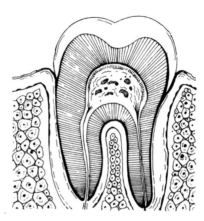

The publishers would like to thank the following artists
for contributing to the book:

Jonathan Adams 18, 36; Andy Archer 66, 80; Mike Atkinson (Garden Studios) 10–11, 12, 34;
Richard Bonson 13, 20–21, 22–23, 30, 31; Kuo Kang Chen 71; Richard Coombes 58–59;
Joanne Cowne (Garden Studios) 34–35; Eugene Fleury 14–15, 36, 51, 65;
Chris Forsey 16–17; Alan Harris 50; Ian Jackson 50, 62, 83;
Roger Kent (Garden Studios) 20, 24–25, 32–33; S Lings 63;
Bernhard Long (Temple Rogers) 66–67; Alan Male (Linden Artists) 36–37, 38–39, 40–41;
Josephine Martin (Garden Studios) 56–57; Bruce Pearson (Wild Life Art Agency) 60–61, 64–65;
Elizabeth Rice (Wild Life Art Agency) 18–19, 26–27, 28–29, 30, 31;
Paul Richardson 72–73, 74–75, 76–77, 78–79; John Ridyard 82;
Eric Robson (Garden Studios) 42–43; Rob Shone 78, 79; Guy Smith (Mainline) 78;
Lucy Su 80, 81, 82, 83; Myke Taylor (Garden Studios) 48–49, 50–51;
Kevin Toy (Garden Studios) 62–63; Guy Troughton 14–15, 52–53, 54–55;
Phil Weare (Linden Artists) 44–45, 46–47, 68–69, 70–71, 80, 81, 82

The publishers wish to thank the following for supplying
photographs for this book:

Page 19 ZEFA; 22 A-Z Botanical; 27 Science Photo Library; 33 Heather Angel; 36 Tony Stone; 37 NHPA Spike
Walker; 41 NHPA George Bernard; 45 ZEFA; 46 NHPA Tony Bannister; 51 Frank Lane Picture Agency; 56
Heather Angel; 60 ZEFA; 62 ZEFA; 65 *t* Bruce Coleman, *c* ZEFA; 73 Allsport; 79 Robert Harding; 80 ZEFA;
83 Helene Rogers/TRIP.